Hire Hotdogs
Fire Baloney

Hiring the Best
Get Praises, Raises,
Promotions and
Fat Profits

by

Don Paullin

ISBN: 0-9785314-0-X

Library of Congress Control Number: 2006927137

Printed in the United States of America
Publication Date: June 2006

Cover design by Angela Farley

Editing and interior book design by Bob Spear

Business Certification Publishing, Inc.
Box 440
Grayslake, IL 60030
847-975-1520
www.HiringFiringExperts.com
Don@HiringFiringExperts.com

Be More Promotable & Increase Profits

Attend or Schedule
Hiring Firing Experts
Presentations, Workshops, Seminars or
Consulting

Go to
www.HiringFiringExperts.com
Or call Don Paullin at 847-975-1520
Or use our convenient order form which follows

Hiring Firing Experts Presentations, Workshops, Seminars and Consulting for Hiring Managers, Owners, and Executives:

"Hiring the Best for Raises, Praises and Profits"—Implement a Hiring System to Hire the Best people for Praises, Raises, Promotions, and Fat Profits. See the pathway to legally and properly Hire and eliminate the fear of lawsuits and EEO audits.

"Fire When Ready"---Fire without Fear with our 6 Step Termination system. Fire with confidence; stay legal and avoid lawsuits.

"Culture Vs. Leadership"---Learn how to achieve a Positive Culture with high employee morale and increased profits.

"Why Do I Act This Way and Why Do They Act So Stupid?"— Understand why you and others act the way they do and how to improve your management skills and persuasiveness when dealing with different personality styles.

Business Opportunity!

Do You Want to Join the Hiring Firing Experts Team and Become a Hiring & Firing Expert?

Have you wanted a great opportunity to own your own business and take charge of your own life? If you have a business background, an entrepreneurial spirit and want to invest in your future then:

Learn what it takes to BECOME ONE of the
Hiring Firing Experts.
Go to:
www.HiringFiringExperts.com
or call 847-975-1520

Become a Certified Hiring Expert!

**Visit www.HiringFiringExperts.com
for information and details.**

**For Book Titles and Other Products go
to page 194**

Acknowledgements

My Hiring Firing System has been a work in process for over twenty years. Thanks to Karen Metropolis for the impetus to complete *Hire Hotdogs Fire Baloney* and to share my Hiring Firing System.

Special thanks to Dick Juntunen for his dedication in working with me on the completion of this book and to Marc Sablo for his creative ideas that added spice to this work. Special appreciation to Vicki Paullin for typing the original manuscript and her helpful editing over the past twenty years.

Thanks to Ken Aldridge owner of Aldridge Electric, Dick Augspurger, Isabel Clop, Angela Farley, Mark Favreau, Judge Gary Neddenriep, Dan Poynter, Al McClendon, Bob Spear, Kristie Tamsevicius and Char Wilson for their critical eyes and ideas.

Thanks to Kevin Breen, Pat Guiney, Ed Kutschke, Doug Holloway, Dawn Ochoa, Devin Paullin, Kathy Sarli and Glen Tullman for their support throughout this project.

Finally, substantial parts of this book were conceived and written in various Starbucks establishments throughout the Chicagoland area and Wisconsin. Thank you Starbucks for the wonderful people and the stayawake coffee.

Table of Contents

PREFACE
When Your Team Sucks
So Do You!

Paullin's Point—People are the number one reason that CEOs, Executives and Managers succeed or fail.

Why Leaders and Companies Fail

The number one reason executives fail is because their Sales Reps do not out sell, their Accountants do not out bean count, their Bidders get outbid, their Engineers are slide rule thinkers and their Marketeers are copying the leaders instead of leading. Leaders fail because of average or poor performing people.

Failing leaders or companies can be traced back to their employees who are average or substandard performers. These leaders do not invest the time to develop and implement a system that gives them championship performers. They do not invest the time in hiring the best. They get what their lack of investment pays for…mediocrity. Hiring championship performers is one step toward greatness; another is firing deadwood. They both must happen.

The Recipe for Being Fired or Being Labeled a Mediocre Manager

If your goal is to be a mediocre manager, then you need not invest in developing your hiring and firing muscles. You may be too busy and rush into your hiring decision. You may hire the candidate who makes you feel good and his average smarts makes you look smart.

On the other hand, if you want to become a productive, promotable, and superstar manager, then invest the time and energy needed to learn how to Hire Champions and Fire Losers. Hiring the best people is the most important role of a superior manager and the vital key to the success of any department or company. If you hire the wrong person, 80% of your job will be staring you in the face every day. If you hire the right person, 80% of your job is behind you and you will sleep well. Bad hires are caffeine pillows and will keep you up at night; good hires are like a pillow promoting restful sleep.

Rising To Your Level of Employee Talent

A quick glance at the Super Bowl shows that both teams are loaded with talent and both coaches look like Super Bowl coaches. The NFL has a history of coaches who have won Super Bowls and have attained Super Coach Status. Later they have been brought down to earth when they have a team of average and marginal players. But when they add Pro Bowl players again, they return to the status of Super Coach. The same can be said of baseball managers and World Series managers. This is an oversimplification, but as a general rule, a coach or manager can only rise to the level of the talent of his players, and this holds true for business executives and managers.

The Top Sales Manager and Mentor Taught Me!

After being promoted to Sales Manager, I set my sights on the next promotion. I selected a mentor whose sales team was consistently in the top 10% in the nation. If I could get my team to the top 20% then I would get promoted. I asked for his help. He said you just need to know one thing—people. He said if you hire hamburger, the best you will ever have is hamburger!

No Buns Hiring

I expanded the theme. Hire hotdogs; pay them well and train them well, and you will have well paid and highly trained baloney in a tube that you must grill. You can't have superior team results that get you raises and praises that feature a menu of hamburger or baloney.

My mentor told me having a team of the best people was all that mattered, nothing else. He said this is accomplished by hiring the best and firing the rest. No matter your position: CEO, Executive, Director or Manager, the fact is that if your career is a result of people productivity then you will be what your team is. If it is a team that sucks, you will suck. If it is a team of average people, then your grade card will be a C. If your team is stocked with championship performers, then you get the praise, the raise, and the accolades of a championship leader.

Sales Reps Fired Four Managers

You are a great Sales Manager as long as your Sales Reps excel—you rise or fall along with their productivity. I turned a sales group from the bottom 10% to the top 10% while working for Searle Pharmaceuticals. This sales group had a history of low productivity, and their last four managers were fired because of poor results. I was determined to turn this group around and get promoted.

> ## *Paullin's Point—You can only be as good a manager as the talent and productivity level of your employees.*

The People Time Bomb Explodes

My mentor's advice was to take the time to upgrade the talent of this low performing sales team—or suck. I up-graded the talent with new hires and eliminated the deadwood performers. I built a team of people whose self-motivation did not permit being average and who were dedicated to becoming championship performers.

Positive Culture of Championship Producers

The results were astounding. Our team won sales contests, got higher raises, and we received the largest bonuses in the company. The company rewarded us by promoting two of my people. They were the first to be promoted in the group in ten years. Everybody was happy, and the team culture was changed positively. The team was nationally noted for their high spirit and results. I got a huge raise, nice bonus and was promoted. The key was my mentor's advice: Focus on one thing—get the best people.

The impetus for this book comes from my mentor's advice and my success in always hiring the best. Through this book, I give you my selection and hiring system so you too can hire the best. I have developed my selection and hiring system over more than twenty years, and it is used by successful managers in large and small companies to identify and hire superior performers. As you read and learn about my selection and hiring system, I believe you too will realize that you can only be as good a manager as the talent and productivity level of your employees.

PART I

Leadership Begins with Great Hires

1

Climb the Ladder of Promotions Without Falling

Managers, Directors and "Rising Stars:" The fastest way to get promoted is to show your CEO or owner that you are the key to increasing his productivity and profits. Producers climb the Promotions Ladder while others partake of the mutual admiration society holding court at the water cooler. The only thing that keeps owners and executive heavies alive at the top are profits and productivity. The best producers will be the people moving up.

It is possible to win the productivity/profits war with just one skill. That skill is team building. Build a team comprised of genuinely self motivated, disciplined, and talented people, and they will bring the culture of positive profits and positive attitudes. People are the core of any business team, and the best people make the best teams. Grabbing the top line on the promotions marquee requires that you have good hiring skills. This book will help you develop hiring muscle. Hiring talent is not a birthright; it is learned wisdom applied.

Owners, CEOs and Bottom Line Feeders

I was an owner and leader of several companies, two of which wound up on the positive side of a NASDAQ IPO. I learned that profit and potential for growth were defining elements for a company needing to be perceived as a "permanent" in business. Anything less than a healthy profit continuum, and your company was viewed as a "wannabe" company and, at best, a short term proposition. Everybody that invests wants to know how they are going to get their money out in the long run. The answer will never be to allow it to run out of the bottom of a badly managed business.

All your employees and capital are at immediate risk when associated with a red bottom-line. The Dot Coms taught the financial community a lesson of profundity not seen since 1929. The Dot Com companies and their failings will be decades at the forefront of the minds of professional and casual investors alike. The essence of their demise was an inability to make money. Business is about making money, and most of them never did. The business universe is back to looking at profits, not hype.

At a certain level your job depends on being a Bottom Line Feeder. Bottom Line Feeders only eat and sleep well when healthy profits abound. Profits are the prophets in the financial world. The best healthy profits exist only when the right team is in place.

Producing the Rings

In the meantime, on the Southside of Chicago, the White Sox have been trying to assemble a winner forever. The problem is not the players but rather the people who pick those players. It is the owners, not the players that are responsible for all championships won or lost. Put the right people in leadership positions, and they will hire the right players to produce the rings.

The Chicago White Sox could not draw a crowd with chalk, but that changed when fans started seeing a potential Would Series winner. The crowds came and paid scalper prices to watch the White Sox win. The White Sox did not win because of their super talented players or their popular Manager of the Year. They won because the owner hired the right GM who hired the players and manager. The team that the GM assembled went from nowhere to waltzing through the playoffs and World Series. The owner is the World Series hero, but few people recognize this phenomenal feat as the hiring of the right team and manager to win the Series.

The White Sox owner's past history demonstrates teambuilding that wins championships. He assembled a team that delivered six NBA championships. It was not Michael Jordan who deserved the credit or should be canonized as the hero of record. It was the owner who was responsible for hiring the managers that hired Jordan and the rest of the players that made up the teams that became NBA Legends and Champions.

The real hero is the owner who was responsible for assembling the entire cast of the champion Bulls and White Sox. Thanks Mr. Reinsdorf.

People Develop the Culture

People who can hire the best talent and manage that talent will put smiles on Bottom Line Feeders. Great managers and great strategies can be derailed, defused, and dispatched by poor producers. It is particularly difficult to lead people who are not self-motivated, so it makes sense to avoid hiring them. We have all met people who are retirees at birth; do not hire them.

Inspired managers and well picked employees foster positive energy and a culture of productivity. Nurture a great culture and it becomes easier to put your plans in effect and to reach goals. A great place to work, raises, praises, promotions and fat profits follow in the wake of a positive culture.

Your Hiring Firing Experts Notes:

2

Turnover Steals More Profits than Fraud and Robbery Combined

> *Paullin's Point—Managers who can state the expense of turnover are likely to manage it. Managers who don't know their turnover cannot manage it.*

Robbing Company Profits without Guns

Fraud and bad hires lose companies big chunks of money that are unseen, but when exposed, the naked figures are a devastating surprise. Fraud gets all the headlines, while bad hires and turnover are more prevalent and damaging to companies' and managers' careers, but far too often, go unnoticed.

Are Your Bad Hires and Turnover Stealing Profits?

Chances are your company has not calculated the costs of a bad hire or turnover and the impact on the bottom line. CEO's, CFO's, and managers who have bottom-line accountability and know the approximate dollar amount of turnover are likely to manage these costs and improve profits. Exposing the naked figures caused by bad hires and turnover will boost profits and make you a hero. Left unexposed, they are profit robbers.

> ## Paullin's Point—Visible Turnover Costs + Hidden Turnover Costs = The Naked Turnover Costs of Bad Hires.

Visible Costs:

Cost of hiring terminated employee $..........................

Cost of training terminated employee $..........................

Salary wasted on days, weeks, or months of terminated employee's negative productivity $.....................

Management hours spent on termination costs $...............

Administrative hours spent on termination costs $.............

Legal support hours spent on termination costs $..............

Cost of hiring terminated person's replacement $.........

Other Visible costs $..

Hidden Costs: (When exposed these are more costly than Visible costs).

The largest amount is opportunity costs or business income lost $...................

Damage done by a bad hire on time and productivity $...............

Damage done by a bad hire with internal and external customers $..............

Cost of infecting employee morale $ ....

Cost for lost sales, Public Relations, etc. $..................................

Cost of the bad hire's mistakes $.............................

Costs of wasting time in correcting errors $...................

Time it takes to get replacement up to speed $............

Other Hidden Costs $...................

Cutting the turnover expense, just as hiring the right people, can dramatically improve the bottom line and profits.

Every Manager Must be Able to State the Expense of Turnover!

The first step is to define the turnover rate as a percentage-for example 20%. Let's assume this 20% gives you an annual turnover rate of twenty people in the sales department. The estimated cost of landing and training a replacement, figuring visible and hidden costs, is $200,000.

The cost of $200,000 X 20 sales reps is $4 million in lost profits. If your organization's profit margin is 10% that means an additional $40 million in sales must be generated to offset this 20% turnover rate!

Manager's Quiz:
1) What is your turnover cost by position?
2) What does your department turnover cost?
3) What is the turnover cost for the company?
4) What amount of sales are needed to cover the cost of turnover?

The Guarantee of Morale, Profits, and Careers

Executives and companies are guaranteed profit problems if turnover expenses are left undefined and unmanaged. The first key to managing turnover costs is to make the best hires as bad hires guarantee high turnover costs. The second key is to get rid of deadwood and replace them with good hires. There is nothing more critical than these two moves to stimulate morale, profits, careers, and this will reduce turnover.

Paullin's Point—When Visible and Hidden costs of bad hires and turnover are calculated they become Nakedly exposed expenses that can be managed.

Your Hiring Firing Experts Notes:

3

Stop the Hiring Lawsuit Fears

Paullin's Point—The lawsuit is won or lost before the filing begins.

Hiring and Firing Systems Win Most Lawsuits by Preventing Them!

Ten laws are listed below which essentially cover seven areas of discrimination. These laws apply to you and your company's policies and actions regarding hiring, performance management, raises, promotions, and firing. Understanding all laws is an overwhelming task, but I will make it easy for you.

Know Ten Laws or Just One Thing!

You need to focus on one simple thing to be in concert with all laws! My safe harbor concept is simple; focus on one thing, the correct job description, and you are likely in concert with all laws and in legal or EEOC compliance. That is it; you only need to stay inside the job description and document for legal compliance to help prevent and possibly win lawsuits.

Employees Win Lotto with Legal Settlements and Judgments

The number of settlements or judgments over $100 million is startling and available to your eyes today on the Internet. The dollars get even more economically devastating because of the expenses in implementing court-imposed affirmative action programs and mounting legal defenses.

Think about the loss of management time, frustration, and reputation of the company when a big EEOC settlement becomes part of the public record.

> ***Paullin's Point—Dollars spent on employment discrimination claims make the cost of developing a hiring, firing and performance appraisal system all based on the job description seem like a penny investment.***

This penny investment will potentially save millions of dollars.

> *It ain't what men don't know that gets them in trouble; it's what they do know that ain't.—Josh Billings, American Humorist*

When you start playing with the legal questions and requirements, just remember what Josh said. I assume everything is illegal if I cannot prove it is job related. I suggest you do the same.

Proven Guilty and Hanging is for Bad Guys, Not for Business People

Sounds a little harsh, given we have always been taught you are innocent until proven guilty. The legal systems in our Constitution are all based on the presumption of innocence.

True or False—You are Innocent Until Proven Guilty? That was true until Congress, in 1991, decided that the employer must prove innocence when charged with employment discrimination suits. Congress decided to add a little extra pain by affording claimants not only compensatory damages but punitive damages as well. Remember you must prove your innocence by proving you are legally compliant and not discriminating. You better have at least a hiring and firing system with documentation to avoid the hangman's compensatory and punitive damage noose.

Many discrimination suits would have never been filed if a job description-based system had been used as the criteria for hiring, firing, promotions, and raises.

Hot Stove Principle: Everybody that touches gets burned the same

Hiring is a necessary event and actually more complicated and frustrating when you do not have a selection system. It is an Equal Employment Opportunity Commission (E.E.O.C.) legal mandate that you must treat all candidates equally. The general rule is that you cannot ask one candidate to be judged for hiring with one set of standards and ask another candidate to be judged for hiring with a different set of standards.

Caught in Court with your "Legal Suit Pants Down"

The good news is essentially the same laws apply to hiring, firing, reviews, and raises. Even better news is simply by focusing on the job description, you will go a long way in being compliant and more likely to stay away from employment discrimination suits. You don't want to be caught in court with your documentation pants down and your job description not showing up.

An Easy Overview of Employment Laws

The Civil Rights Act of 1964

Title VII of this act pertains to employment and prohibits discrimination because of:

Race
Color
Sex or Gender
Religious Beliefs
National Origin

The Age Discrimination in Employment Act (amended 1978)

Prohibits discrimination from Age 40 and over.

The Rehabilitation Act of 1973

Prohibits job discrimination against individuals with disabilities who are otherwise qualified. Applies to federal

---

government, government contractors, and recipients of federal financial assistance.

The Vietnam Era Veterans Readjustment Assistance Act of 1974

Protects employment rights of disabled and qualified veterans of the Viet Nam era. Applies to federal government, government contractors and recipients of federal financial assistance.

The Pregnancy Discrimination Act of 1978

Amended Title VII to add pregnancy and childbirth.

The Immigration Reform and Control Act of 1986

Prohibits the employment of any alien not authorized to work and requires two forms of identification as proof of authorization to work.

Equal Pay Act of 1963

Requires that men and women performing substantially equal work be paid equally.

The Americans with Disabilities Act of 1990

Prohibits discrimination against individuals with disabilities. All non-essential job activities must be eliminated from job descriptions and in selection decisions. Reasonable accommodation must be made if it is not an economic hardship for employer.

The Civil Right Act of 1991

The burden of proof is placed on employers in cases of discrimination and permits compensatory and punitive damages in civil trials.

Family and Medical Leave Act of 1993

Allows up to 12 weeks of unpaid leave in a 12-month period for: Birth, adoption, foster care of child; care for child, spouse or parent; or because of one's own health condition.

Making It Easy For Managers and Companies

The laws are numerous, and coupled with all the scenarios, are an ambitious task to weave into your hiring system. A simpler way is to work everything you do off of the job description. For legal compliance, simply stay with the job description for your hiring, firing, performance appraisals, raises, and promotions.

There are two important reasons not to ask any questions that are prejudicial in these areas. One: It is illegal and will get you into major league trouble. Two (and maybe the most important to your company's bottom line): You may knock out the person who could perform best and who would make you look like a superior manager.

Do You Wonder if What You are Doing is Legal?

The good news is you do not have to be a lawyer to figure out what questions are illegal. **If you wonder if it is illegal…chances are it is.** If you have any doubts about the question discriminating forget the question. You will generally stay out of problems if you just make sure that all your questions are job related and equal for all people.

The Uncomplicated Acid Test

There is a long list of illegal areas that you cannot question. Now for the list of areas in which you can develop questions: you should develop questions that are job related. Yes, you have it, a list of one— questions that are job related. This is the *acid test* and this removes the complication.

I know somebody will say there are some exceptions to the rules called bona fide occupational qualifications (BFOQ's) from Title VII of the Civil Rights Act. My advice is forget them unless you have a bona fide legal defense fund.

Let's do an EEOC test that I made up for an exercise in legality.
How many children do you have?
(Discriminates against women)

Are you married?
(Discriminates against women)

Have you ever been arrested?
(Person may have not been convicted)
Do you have a college degree?

(You had better be able to prove that a college degree is essential to performing the job. The facts are that you can seldom prove this, and usually there are people who have performed that job without a degree. You can prefer a college degree. You can, however, require a medical degree for a doctor, a law degree for a lawyer and so forth because people in these types of professions cannot do the job without the appropriate degree.)

When did you graduate from high school or college?
(Age discrimination)

This job requires that you lift 200-pound bales of hay. Will that be a problem?
(OK, only if it is job related such as stacking bails of hay on a farm.)

Will you work the Sunday morning shift?
(OK, only if it is job related and applied fairly to all regardless of religion.)

I will now weasel word out of the above test and tell you that it may or may not be correct, but it will cause you to think and decide on the safe side. The fact is if you are not sure of a question, there are plenty of good questions to compose, so write another one that is perfectly job related and legal. (I provide you with over 300 job related questions.)

I am not an attorney; I work for a living. This book is not legal advice but only my opinion. Consult an attorney for legal advice. When interviewing, the ball is in your court and the courtroom will be your ballroom if your questions can be construed as discriminatory. Remember what humorist Josh Billings said, because you must prove your innocence.—Don Paullin

Your Best Defense

Designing and implementing a proper selection system will provide you the best hires and may mean not saying you're sorry for a big verdict against you and your company. Your properly designed and legally compliant system may payoff in high dividends of productivity, profits, the best people, and winning the legal war without fighting the battles.

4

Bet On the Jockey, Not the Horse

Paullin's Point—If you are a manager, you are not what you eat but what you hire.

Millions are Bet on the Jockeys

Most bettors bet on the horse not the jockey. In contrast, Venture Capital tends to put its money on the management team rather than the product. **They bet millions on the "jockeys" or management team to build great companies.** Nothing will build a great company faster than the best managers hiring the best teams. People are the single best ingredient to the success of marketing, sales, operations, accounting, research, and all the other corporate functions. The best hires ride the company productivity to winning careers, raises, and profits.

You're fired!

If you want to correct a company or a department that seems to feature lazy, unmotivated, and low productivity performers, then fire or train the incompetents. It is not the slackers or unmotivated employees who are the incompetents, but rather the managers of the poor producers who hired the substandard performers and continue to employ them. Unmotivated employees and substandard producers will fire the manager and ruin the company that keeps them because of their poor performance.

> *Paullin's Point—Unmotivated employees, when hired to majority, will fire the manager and the company that retains them through poor performance and bankruptcy.*

Not firing directly damages four people:

The person holding the job who shouldn't and is miserable

The talented person who wants the job and can't have it until the low performer is fired

The manager who fails to terminate the substandard performer and lives with the problem

The boss of the manager looks bad too.

You can have the newest and best widget and, as a general rule, your company will fail if you do not stock it with superior players. If your salespeople do not outsell, if your bean counters do not watch the beans, if your production people do not optimize production, even the best widget designer is funeralized.

> *Paullin's Point—A company's life or death is in the hands of its hired hands.*

Conversely, the history books of business are filled with success stories of average products that have come to the market late, but armed with superior people, have battled their way to the top of the marketplace. I believe that an average product with superior management will beat a superior product managed by average people about 96% of the time.

Paullin's Profit Hiring Grid
Superior Hires = Superior Managers = Superior Profits
Average Hires = Average Managers = Average Profits
Bad Hires = Bad Managers = Bad Profits

Summary

So Doubting Thomas', if you do not believe, then watch the court of Venture Capitalists as they pronounce their verdicts and cash rewards. People who come into the Venture Capitalist court seeking their monies find that an excellent product represented by unproven management tends to receive no funding. They are advised to find experienced managerial talent with proven and successful track records to gain the money. An average product backed by proven management winners will get the verdict and the gold. The Venture Capital gamblers bet their money on the Jockey, not the Horse.

Paullin's Point—Bad hires are like hemorrhoids; they are a pain in the butt and must be medicated or removed.

Your Hiring Firing Experts Notes:

5

The "Curse of Nimble Jones"

Great Managers begin with Great Hires
Great Hires make Great Companies
Great Companies make Great Profits
Great Profits make Great Raises
Out with the Curse of Nimble Jones

The **"Curse of Nimble Jones"** is a short story and is must reading by all those holding the following executive ID cards: Owners, CEO's, Presidents, and ladder climbers who aspire to be Managers or Executives.

Why are we Average?

This is the story of Nimble Jones the owner of a company that reached number one in market share and was considered by all to be a superlatively managed company. Some years later, the company descended from number one to an average company.

Nimble knew he had a superior product and knew his original talented managers put his company at the top as the market leader. Over time, his number one company armed with the superior product was managed from first to a middle market position. Nimble was disheartened and shocked because Nimble had a superior product line and paid his people the highest wages. However, the company now underperformed and wallowed in mediocrity.

Money, pay, products, and the marketing plan all pointed to the company being Number One. Why had the company's performance fallen to disappointingly average? Nimble Jones searched for the answer.

Nimble met with his managers and asked, "Why are we average?" None of the managers would tell him why. He was frustrated because his managers were clearly the most talented in the industry. He remembered Ralph who had hired the managers that led the company to the status of being number one. He asked Ralph what the problem was and Ralph said that he could not tell Nimble why.

Nimble went to all managers, supervisors and employees to find the answer to the company's mediocrity. All agreed that their managers and bosses were people who knew their jobs. But none could come up with the answer for the mediocrity.

The Great Consultant Guru

Nimble turned to the Great Consultant Guru who quickly charged him a lot of money but had all the answers. The Great Consultant Guru said the problem was coming from bad management Karma; "don't hire such great talent that they look smarter than you."

In the beginning Ralph had hired the best people and touted their skills and the company performance rose to number one. Nimble promoted Ralph's hires above Ralph and Ralph's name was removed from those being considered for promotion to the President's list. Ralph's successful hiring of championship performers had in a strange way diminished Ralph's deserved career path to President.

The managers Ralph hired saw what happened to Ralph and all vowed to not make the "Ralph Mistake." So the managers Ralph hired learned to make good hires instead of great hires! Hires were not to be so good that they looked better than their boss. The perception was that if you make great hires and talk them up, they would get promoted ahead of you as seen with Ralph. This perception is alive today in many companies and this phenomenon is known as "**Dummy Down Hiring**" or the **"Curse of Nimble Jones"**.

The "Great" Ralph

Ralph was a great manager and one of his key strengths was hiring superstar managers and the superstars helped propel the company performance to number one. This should have caught Nimble's attention and then Nimble would have promoted Ralph to be President. Everybody in the company, except Nimble, saw the company reach number one because of Ralph's superior hires. More importantly, they saw that Nimble did not promote Ralph but rather the people Ralph hired. The

"**Curse of Nimble Jones**" was reinforced and embedded in all of Nimble's managers.

The "**Curse of Nimble Jones**" if found in a company must be removed for morale, promotions, productivity and profits. The remedy is found in the Great Consultant Guru's advice: The executive must communicate that every manager's goal is to hire the best even if they are better than the hiring manager. Superior hires will result in the highest productivity and profits. Managers who hire the best will be promoted.

Hire the best because the axiom that you can't be promoted unless you can be replaced is internalized. Also, managers must terminate substandard performers—this means, "Managers must whack'em and stack'em by chopping out the deadwood."

The combination of communicating and rewarding managers for best hire practices will result in superior company productivity and profits. Best hire practices are the keys to promotions and raises.

The leader must communicate the "**Curse of Nimble Jones**" to all managers throughout the organization.

Your Hiring Firing Experts Notes:

6

Dummy Down Hiring

How to Sabotage a Company's Culture and Kill Profits

Dummy Down hiring as we saw in the **"Curse of Nimble Jones"** is caused by the misdirection of leadership. Leadership must come with a message and dedication to review and promote the managers who hire the best. The misdirection comes from promoting the great hires over the managers who hire them. The message must not be, "hire good people but not so good as to show you up." To prevent Dummy Down Hiring, praise and raise the great hires, but also praise and raise the managers who continue to hire the best.

> *Paullin's Point—Your performance as a manager is not how you perform, but how your team performs.*

Summary
Like a football or baseball team, your performance is measured by your team's productivity in wins and losses. If you want to become a superior manager invest the time and energy needed to learn how to Hire Champions and Fire Losers. Successfully doing this is your most important role and is vital to your success, the success of your department and the success of the company.

Your Hiring Firing Experts Notes:

PART II

Positive Cultures are Deliberate not Accidents

7

Company Clutter and The Closet Organizer

Clutter-spasm—the Recipe for Clutter Depression

Have you ever had or seen a case of clutter depression? Just keep building clutter in your car, clutter the trunk, the seats, and especially clutter the floorboard. Many people prefer to clutter their house, clutter the closets, the garage, and even neatnicks find it easy to clutter the basement. You will soon feel the negative energy sapping power of Clutter-spasm.

Usually stuff insidiously builds up and slowly dominates your space until it is classified as clutter. People do not react to the clutter phenomenon until they reach the threshold of pain that becomes so intolerable that the clutter becomes junk. When you hit the clutter pain threshold you will start throwing away junk and will lose control of your "stop throwing away sensors." In the absence of "stop throwing away sensors," everything is thrown away with vigor.

Once you begin throwing away clutter an immediate feeling of empowerment takes over. Your muscles work faster tossing clutter fueled by an adrenalin clutter rush. Soon the phenomenon known as Clutter-gasm shoots through your mind and body.

My first Clutter-gasm took My Son

I once decluttered one of my homes after twenty years of clutter build up. I hit the clutter pain threshold as the clutter became junk. I put giant industrial bins on the driveway for clutter fill-up that would be hauled away by special trucks. I was filling my fifth bin when the adrenalin clutter rush hit and the endorphin high put me into total throw away warp three. I started throwing away the stuff that I had saved for some occasion that never came and that is when I hit the clutter euphoric feeling. I became so addicted to the clutter tossing euphoria, I could not stop tossing stuff.

I think it was the screaming of "Daddy" that brought me back to reality. I was embarrassed as I retrieved my 8 year old son who I accidentally tossed in the bin. He quickly explained that he was not clutter but my son. It was hard for me to explain to him that for one brief second of clutter tossing I had mistaken him for a statue lamp. I apologized, dusted him off, took him to a Chicago Bears game, and all was forgiven.

Clutter Culture

Clutter culture is an insidious growth cancer inside a company. It is simply a matter of sub par performers allowed to stay cluttering up a company. Clutter people seem to do enough to just hang on to their jobs until they become the unsightly junk on a company that can't be hidden.

Negative Culture

Negative-people-clutter comes with clutter chatter which is the negative water-cooler talk that kills morale. At this stage, negative people focus on what is wrong with their company, co-workers, and their bosses rather than their own productivity. Negative clutter cultures can be changed by simply eliminating the people who whine rather than produce. They should be replaced by hungry people wanting to do the job because of self motivation. You can turn negative culture into positive culture.

Positive Culture

Positive Culture is so much fun and people say, "I love my job, my company is the greatest, and my boss has taught me a lot." Their company talk is so positive that others want to work for you. These employees don't hate Mondays and they will stay late to get things done. I don't really need to explain positive culture further—you will know it.

> *When you have a positive culture, all else follows: People make money, the company makes money, people get promoted, and the Cubs may even win the World Series.—Ken Aldridge, CEO Aldridge Electric*

Clutter-gasm

Hire the best people; put the right people in the right jobs; fire the substandard performers; silence the negative talkers; create an environment for growth; and you will experience the rewards of a Positive Culture. Clutter-gasm is the pleasure that is enjoyed when you turn a company around from Clutter-spasm or Negative Culture into a Positive Culture. If you have done it, then you will know the satisfaction of conquering one of the most formidable business challenges.

Your Hiring Firing Experts Notes:

8

Culture—The People Pearls to Grow a Jewel of a Company

> *"Culture Eats Strategy for Breakfast;" any strategic plan, no matter how valuable, will not happen without commitment from the highest and most effective people in the firm.—Author Unknown*

Culture an oyster and a pearl will develop just like an ocean pearl which is naturally grown by live oysters. The guiding hand of the oyster farmer adds an element of culturing and motivation for the oyster. This is more efficient than a grain of sand finding the oyster shell in the ocean. Culture management makes optimum conditions for the live oyster to grow the perfect pearls that make the valued jewel necklace.

Pearls make necklaces, and people are the pearls of great companies. Culture is again the first step in making a valuable company and developing the right people. People pearls are grown from the culture and make the company desirable to employees, owners, and customers.

Pearls Make the Necklace and People Make the Company

My good friend, Ken Aldridge, told me that if you develop the culture of a company all else will follow. His wholly owned $200 million company is a leading national electrical contractor. His philosophy of culture first and everything else will come naturally gave me the analogy of the pearl necklace and people pearls.

Tarnished Pearls Ruin Value
If the silk thread breaks, the Pearls are lost on the ground

One of their biggest problems CEOs and owners tell me, is that some of their people are negative and start to weaken the invisible string that holds the pearl necklace together. These successful leaders know their companies but the people problems are keeping them awake at night and dumping acid into their stomachs. In talking with executives, we define the problem as the culture has turned south with some of the pearls tarnishing the necklace.

Going back to the analogy of the pearl necklace and people pearls, if the silk thread breaks, the pearls are scattered. A good culture provides the cohesiveness that holds the pearls together; it is the string that secures the strand. It is reasonable to equate culture with the oyster, and a company's strategic mission or plan to the grain of sand.

Cultured pearls are not random but deliberate efforts at beauty, quality, productivity and repeatability. Cultured pearls are man's attempt at improving the goodness of nature. For companies, the analogy applies. Instead of letting fortunate accidents birth the employee people pearls, why not create a positive culture and afford training and opportunity so employees evolve into beautiful people pearls. Those fortunate accidents cannot be counted on but the formulation of a solid culture and attendant strategic plans can.

I think the culture of a company means developing people and creating a positive growth environment. When added to a customer driven mission, this benefits all. The right messages with the right pearls in place create the culture from the owner passed on to the team. Add the proper culture, and the employees become pearls that make a jewel of a company.

PART III

Why Paullin's Hiring Firing Experts System

9

The Six Most Painful Moments in Interviewing and the Pain Killers

The Value of the Predictor Interview Guide

This chapter on Pain and the Pain Killers is sponsored by the Hiring Firing Experts **Predictor Interview Guides**. It stresses the reasons for designing **Predictor Interview Guides** and why you will love using the **Guides**.

Key Benefits of Predictor Interview Guides are:
Usually saves 1-3 hrs of time per candidate
Helps you stay legal and EEOC compliant
Alleviates frustration and embarrassment
Provides documentation
Enhances your memory
You are perceived as a prepared interviewer
Your company is perceived as even more professional
You have better hires and better profits

Pain #1—No time to prepare for the interview:

You walk into your office after a meeting with the boss, and somebody is sitting in your office. Woops! Who could this person be? "Hi, I am Susan Ontime, and you scheduled me for a 10 am interview. I flew in

37

from Maine, and I am on time and ready for my interview!" Many times you will have little time to prepare for an interview and will just panic.

Pain! The candidate is waiting; you were busy, and you are now embarrassingly unprepared!

The Painkiller:

Relax and reach for your prepared painkiller; the **Predictor Interview Guide** will always save your hide. It is custom-made for that specific job description and is also designed to help keep you legally and EEOC compliant. Simply open your drawer, pull out your **Predictor Interview Guide** for that job description, and ask Ms. Ontime for a copy of her resume. Now you are prepared with the proper questions for that specific job description, complete with space for recording answers and the evaluation scale. The **Predictor Interview Guide** will help keep you on the legal pathway of proper questions; plus, it works as your necessary legal documentation. You have the flexibility of adding questions to the guide that come to your mind or not asking questions from the guide that you don't need. The **Predictor Interview Guide** is custom designed for a better interview. This makes interviewing easier for you and helps keep you EEOC compliant. After you have finished the interview, save the guide with your recorded notes for EEOC documentation.

Pain #2—Confusion over which candidate is which:

You meet with the other team interviewers to discuss and evaluate the five candidates you have interviewed that day.

Pain! You had a marketing meeting, six phone calls, a discussion of your performance with your boss, a vendor presentation, and interviews with five key candidates.

Pain! You can't remember which candidate did what. Which one was the salesperson of the year? Which one was the scratch golfer?

The Painkiller:

The magic memory enhancer. As you interviewed each candidate, you took good notes over the job-related questions, immediately evaluated each candidate after the interview, graded them, and marked the evaluation scale in your **Predictor Interview Guide**. Reviewing your **Predictor Interview Guide** notes and the guide's evaluation scale will quickly bring you back to the specific candidates. This is proven to refresh your memory on who accomplished what and who did not. If it does not, then tone down your day when you are interviewing, and always limit interviewing to three to four people. Increase your dosage of gingko, if you can remember where you put the gingko!

Pain #3—Candidate says, "Will I get the job?" What do I say?

I know that I will not give the job to this candidate.

Pain: The candidate just asked me if he is going to get the job, and if not, why not?

More Pain! He also fits a protected class category. I'm on the spot, what can I tell him?

The Memorized Painkiller:

Don't panic; you have the memorized Painkiller Line. You have interviewed him with only job-related questions and recorded notes into your **Predictor Interview Guide** with your evaluation scores. You have been EEOC compliant and have documentation. You comfortably say, *"We will be interviewing several candidates and making our evaluations. If you have not heard from us by (supply day or date), that probably means that you will not get the job."* Thank him, stand up, and shake his hand with good-bye body language. If he repeats his question, you smile and repeat your answer.

Pain #4—Calling the wrong reference without permission:

EXPLAIN COSTLY PAIN TO THE BOSS AND THIS MISTAKE COULD COST YOU YOUR JOB! You are proudly doing your due diligence, as your boss requested, by calling reference checks from the candidate's *former* employers. You call the current employer by mistake. You tell him that you are thinking of hiring Dick Jones and would he give Dick a reference? He indicates surprise at Dick seeking another job and answers NO! But he will immediately have a talk with Dick about his current job and his status.

Woops, big Pain Mistake! You called the wrong reference, without the candidate's permission, and this could spell lawsuit and real trouble.

More Pain! You must explain this costly mistake to your boss!

And Even More Pain! You could be fired for such a mistake!

The Painkiller:

Never fear... The Hiring Firing Experts system is designed to prevent calling by mistake. The system has you ask the candidate whom he reported directly to at various jobs. Once the name is given, you ask the candidate if he would give you permission to use the manager as a reference. If yes, only then do you ask for the phone number of the specific manager being discussed. You only record numbers that the candidate gives you with permission to call. This way you have a system that never allows a reference call unless the candidate gives you permission to make the call. This is all recorded in your **Predictor Interview Guide**. You don't ever look-up phone numbers and only use numbers given with permission and written in your guide. Thus, the **Predictor Interview Guide** provides documentation, forces the candidate to be more truthful, and helps uncover the lying candidate.

Pain #5—The multi-million dollar pain:

Your lawyer calls announcing a possible lawsuit for EEOC discrimination. She explains that the burden of proof of innocence is on you and your company. She states that if you have been EEOC compliant with the job description and supply the proper documentation, she will likely have the suit quickly dismissed.

Money Pain! You state you really do not have documentation and that you really assumed this would not happen to you and your company. *Besides, you and your managers hire by their gut feelings!* You have an upset stomach that gut medicines won't touch.

The Painkiller:

No guts, lots of glory! You have an entire interviewing system that supplies all the documentation based on job description interviewing. Your system contains an evaluation scale that treats all candidates the same. This helps provide proof of EEOC compliance. Your attorney replies, *"Great system and documentation,"* and it is likely an early dismissal dream. She compliments you in front of the CEO, President, and the World, as she states, *"He who has the most paperwork wins."* You get promoted, praises, and a raise!

Pain #6—Their credentials—fact or fiction:

It is widely known that a large percentage of candidates lie about degrees because people are just too busy to check. Your president draws to your attention that a friend of his from Harvard informed him that he did not believe the candidate you just hired really has a Harvard MBA. Your boss asks, *"How did your verify the MBA?"*

Embarrassed face with reddening pain! You accept responsibility and explain that you did not check, but are now on it. You are told to verify the degree, and if the candidate lied, you must fire him immediately for falsification and lack of integrity.

The Painkiller:

It's easy and takes the time burden off your back! Ask the candidate if he would request his university to send an official transcript to you and let you know when you might expect it. If the candidate does not follow-through, that is how he will perform on follow-through on the job and you don't want him. If the candidate did get caught in a lie, he and the transcript will likely not show up.

A reminder on requesting the transcript and or degree is on the interview guide with the candidate's commitment. Your **Predictor Interview Guide** becomes documentation that this information was requested and provides the date of the request.

Paullin's Point—In addition to copies of transcripts and degrees, appropriate certificates and licenses, ask the candidate for company reference telephone numbers, home and cell numbers, performance appraisals, and anything that in your good judgment the candidate can properly handle. The candidates' time is free until you hire them, and this relieves you of the time burdens.

Your Hiring Firing Experts Notes:

10

Paullin's 12-Step No Sweat Hiring System

Hiring Can Be Easy Or:

Hiring can become a nightmare for managers without an effective and understandable selection system. It is also hazardous to a company's health to not have a legally compliant selection system. Remember, under U.S. law all candidates must be treated equally. As a general rule, you cannot ask one candidate to be judged for hiring with one set of standards, and ask another candidate to be hired by a different set of standards.

Without an effective and understandable selection system a company's managers will waste time reinventing the selection process. This ends-up with a poor interviewing process, possible selection of inferior employees, and potentially illegal hiring decisions.

Outcomes of a Poor Selection System:
  Incomplete data for decision making
  Illegal questions and potential lawsuits
  Enormous time wasting
  Out walk good candidates
  Everybody feels bad
  Bad impression of you and the company

IT Can Be Easy and Rewarding

An effective, understandable and compliant selection system will bring high dividends in the payoff of great people and profits. Here is **Paullin's 12-Step No Sweat Hiring System.** It is introduced here and the chapters that follow elaborate on each step.

> ***Paullin's Point—If you don't invest the time to do it correctly today, you will spend more time and money in repairing mistakes tomorrow.***

Paullin's 12-Step No Sweat Hiring System

Step 1...Writing the Job Description

Decide What You Need to Hire. A fundamental mistake that managers make in hiring is right at the beginning of the selection process by not having a clear documented description of what the job is all about. Without the job description the manager cannot design a proper advertisement, provide the search firms job and candidate specifications, give information to candidates, or even write proper interviewing questions.

The job description is your guide in writing your advertisement, designing your interview questions, communicating to candidates, and evaluating candidates. It is the essential guiding light for search firms. The job description is a must for proper legal defense! It is the essential tool to give to search firms and managers involved in the hiring process.

A job description captures the scope and purpose of the job. Its format customarily consists of: the job title; a general summary; principal duties and responsibilities; and the knowledge, skills and abilities required to perform the job.

The job description is an essential part of my hiring system. All hiring decisions are based on tools and questions derived from the properly written job description. In **Chapter 11** I've provided a job description example which will help you learn to accurately write up-to-date descriptions for the jobs you are recruiting.

Step 2...Job Predictors

Job Predictors are job performance traits that predict expected, specific job performance. The Predictors that you select are those that are most important to the job. They are the necessary traits of job performance on which a conclusion for making the best hire can be based. These are best determined from the job description as well as from employees who have held the position or managed the position. Based on my experience, I have defined and listed more than 30 Job Predictors most often used in my hiring system. You may define your own Predictors that are key to your positions. The Predictors are your keys to hiring the best and link the job description to the hiring tools presented in this book. Job Predictors are discussed in **Chapters 15, 16 and 17**.

Step 3...Recruiting

> ### *Paullin's Point—If there are only minnows in the pond, you can't catch a trophy fish regardless of the bait.*

When it comes to hiring the best, the same logic applies. You must develop an applicant pool that has the depth to provide a choice of quality candidates. Your applicant pool can come from a number of sources both external and internal to your company.

External advertising, through commercial, professional, government, and school alumni job posting and web-based sites, can be used. Employment agencies and executive search firms may provide good value and increase your pool.

Employee referrals are highly regarded and have traditionally proven to be a reliable source of quality candidates. In tight labor markets, incentives can be paid to employees for successful referrals. Often, part of the incentive is paid when the candidate comes on board and the remainder is paid after they have been employed beyond a certain length of time.

Candidates can apply directly to companies via their job opportunity boards found on the company websites. Another inexpensive source of high quality talent comes by way of outplacement firms and via the many networking groups for people in job transition. These exist in communities throughout the country.

Networking itself can be effective by letting the people you do business with, and the people you've dealt with in the past, know about your job opening.

A company's internal job posting or job opportunity system taps the internal candidate pool. The internal job opportunity system is often the cornerstone of a company's promotion from within philosophy and a key part of a company's culture.

There are a number of ways to develop a high quality candidate pool, and this pool is the only way you will be able to hire the best. See **Chapters 12, 13 and 14**.

Step 4...Resume Screening

Screaming or Screening! Wasting time is killing success. Proper resume screening is a great time saver and prevents the urge to scream when you are handed a pile of 500 resumes. The skill here is to know how to properly read a resume while keeping in mind that a resume is like a movie trailer which only shows the good scenes. So in addition to determining whether the candidate meets your job requirements and specifications, you need to be able to evaluate the resume on both what it does and does not say. By skillfully screening resumes you can determine those who you really want to TeleScreen. **Chapter 19** shows how.

Step 5...TeleScreening

Phone It In! After the resume screen, proper telephone or TeleScreening will save time and frustration. You will learn how to write your TeleScreen with job related questions using a preformatted TeleScreen guide. This ensures defensible decisions because you consistently ask the same questions. Your TeleScreen includes a closing statement which also helps ensure legal compliance and defensibility. Most importantly, your TeleScreen allows you to knock out candidates and prioritize the good ones that you will invite in for face-to-face interviews.

Your TeleScreen can be written and used as a 10-minute phone screen. This will save you hours of time and acid-producing frustration in writing phone screens for every candidate. This is thoroughly described in **Chapter 20** and an example TeleScreen form is shown in **Chapter 30**.

Step 6...The Predictor Interview Guide

Being Prepared Puts Your Best Foot Forward. You are the primary impression the interviewee has of the company so you must look organized and prepared. The Predictor Interview Guide is the most valuable tool in selecting the best candidate, staying legally compliant, and giving the candidate the most positive impression of you, management, and the company.

From your TeleScreens you have decided on whom to interview. You are now ready to write your Predictor Interview Guide. As with the TeleScreen, you write the Predictor Interview Guide with job-related questions. You do this by using the job description as your platform. Use the candidate's resume and background to make the interview questions candidate specific.

Predictor Interview Guides are explained in **Chapter 18** and an example Predictor Interview Guide is shown in **Chapter 30**.

Step 7…The Initial Interview

You are the hiring manager, and you now invite the candidates in for their first round interviews. I recommend you conduct this first round by yourself. This way you are determining those who will be invited back for second round interviews with your colleagues.

An important interview skill is controlling the interview. This does not mean having a Theory X domineering style in the interview. It means asking only the proper questions and listening to answers. It means if the candidate is generalizing, you bring him or her back to specifics and more succinct answers. Along with being armed with questions based on Predictors, this allows you to maintain your focus on the candidate's past job related experiences and keep the candidate focused on answering your interview questions. By doing this you can obtain the data you need to make a good hiring decision.

In **Chapters 21, 22 and 23** you will learn how to separate the well qualified candidate from the smooth talking con and people who wander or ramble through their answers. You will also learn the 75% rule of listening, a very powerful and too often forgotten interviewing tool that causes the candidate to share even more information. You will see how the effective use of open-ended and follow-up questions to probe and obtain information gives you even more decision making information. You will also see how to professionally end the interview in a way that helps ensure legal compliance and defensibility of your selection decision.

Step 8…Reference Checking as a Company Policy

The Insurance Policy that Pays Before You Crash. You wouldn't think of driving without an insurance policy so don't hire without a New Hire Insurance Policy. You may have heard that nobody will give references—wrong! Reference checks are obtainable and essential. Reference checks are your insurance policy that will help prevent costly mistakes in turnover and problems.

Many consultants place this later in the selection sequence. I prefer that it be done before team interviewing and think of it as the Validator vs. Terminator. Reference checks should provide validation of the candidate or may provide termination of further consideration.

In **Chapter 24** you will learn the proper way to obtain references from your candidates and the proper way to successfully conduct them. Most importantly you will understand the value of reference checks. A TeleReference example is shown in **Chapter 30.**

Step 9...Team Interviewing

Three heads are better than one. Team interviewing with 3 managers is essential when interviewing for managerial positions and often is a good idea for professional positions. **This means 3 managers (2 others and you) interview the candidate individually**. Each interviewer is armed with Predictor questions written up in their Predictor Interview Guides. Each interviewer then confirms and validates past job performance which will predict success in the open position. Job offers are critical decisions and the team process works better for "go/no-go" decisions. For lower level positions, where a person only completes an application and does not have a resume, you may need just one person interviewing.

> *Paullin's Point—If the job requires a resume, then have three people individually interview the candidate. If it only requires an application one or two people may be sufficient.*

In **Chapter 25** you will see how the assessments of more than one interviewer help provide reliability and validity to the selection decision through the team interviewing process.

Step 10...Team Data Sharing and Decision Time

Avoid the Gunfight at Ego Corral. Avoid fist fights and fast draw contests by checking all the egos and guns at the door through the structured team data sharing process. If the head boss interviews I recommend it be understood that the "boss hat" comes off during the data sharing meeting.

Each Interviewer's Predictor scores from each candidate's Predictor Interview Guide go into the Predictor Score Card. This provides the basis for the interviewers to discuss the scores on each Predictor and at the conclusion of the discussion reach a final score for the candidate on that specific Predictor.

Team data sharing is detailed in **Chapter 25** as well as an example of a completed Predictor Score Card.

Step 11...Job Offer

You Win! Having followed the Twelve Step No Sweat Hiring System, by the time you make the job offer, everything you have done should give you a certain comfort that your offer will be accepted. This becomes not only a time of anticipation but an occasion for joyous celebration. Let the candidate know they beat a lot of people and were selected as best for the job.

This step is no less important than any other. Remember, the candidate is still evaluating you and may be weighing your offer against others. Make sure you handle this step with class and confidence because you are representing yourself and your company. You don't want to let the "Big One" get away.

Chapter 27 on closing the deal gives you the fine points to help you ensure success.

Step 12...On-Boarding

Victory Flag and Trophy. Your new hire now has accepted your offer and is coming on board. This is your victory, and you want to make your new employee feel he or she is the trophy. It is here you acquaint and accessorize your new employee. Make sure the orientation exceeds what you would expect for yourself. Make sure your new hire has all the tools, equipment, and work space required to begin contributing immediately and to feel really good about being here.

Memorialize! This is your opportunity to introduce and make your new employee part of the company's culture. In doing this, you are reselling them on the company and their future.

On-boarding in a first class way is an essential ingredient for the employee's retention and success. **Chapter 28** gives you many ideas on how to make on-boarding a first class experience and make your new hire feel they are a real member of the organization.

Beyond the 12 Steps

Call Your Attorney before the Doctor! A medical physical may be appropriate after the job offer. Passing the physical then may be documented as a condition of employment. Drug testing and the medical physical should be in written guidelines, and by all means, reviewed and approved by your attorney.

Letters of Rejection. My rejection letters are letters of Appreciation but Still Searching, or A.S.S. letters. These letters can be sent out at different stages in the system or at the end. You'll see my philosophy on letters of rejection with an example in **Chapter 26**.

You don't need a Humvee to go to Starbucks. You may wish to modify your selection system depending on the skill and salary level of the position. It is your system; redesign it as needed to fit your particular needs. You don't need a Humvee to go to Starbucks. You should not use the same resources for a $25,000 a year position that you would for a $100,000 a year position.

I believe the remainder of this book will give you the knowledge, ideas, and tools to hire the best. I also believe, that as I discovered, you will discover too that **great managers begin with great hires**.

PART IV

Paullin's Hiring Firing Experts System

11

Writing the Job Description

The starting point and roadmap for hiring the best

You Have it All in Your Head

Why should you write a job description? You're too busy. You have a department to run. What's more important, delivering results or spending time on something administrative like writing a job description? So just run an ad, forget the job description, and get some people in you can talk to.

Decide What You Need to Hire

Having an up-to-date and current job description is the important starting point of your hiring system. Thinking that writing or updating a job description is just an administrative task could not be further from the truth. An up-to-date and current job description is the foundation for successful hiring, ongoing performance management and if necessary firing.

Defining the job in writing enables you to determine and communicate the overall purpose of the job; the job's principal duties and responsibilities; and the knowledge, skills, abilities, background and experience the candidate needs to perform the job.

The properly written job description is the basis for:
- Writing your advertisement
- Designing interview questions and Interview Guides
- Communicating position requirements to managers

- Communicating position requirements to search firms
- Communicating position requirements and expectations to candidates
- Communicating position level and reporting relationships
- TeleScreening, interviewing and evaluating candidates
- Measuring competing candidates
- Legally defending your hiring decision
- Measuring ongoing performance

Key job description elements are:
I. Job Title Section
In addition to the job title, this section may include other job identification information such as department name, location, and job grade or level.

II. Job Summary
This is a general summary or job purpose statement. Most companies limit this to one or two concise paragraphs.

III. Principal Duties and Responsibilities
This is a comprehensive listing of the position's major tasks and responsibilities (It is not however intended to list all conceivable tasks). This list may indicate duties and responsibilities in some priority order.

IV. Knowledge, Skills and Abilities
These are the preferred and required levels of knowledge, skills and abilities to adequately perform the job.

V. Other job description data
a) Scope Data
For example: Budget, sales, profit responsibilities; number of people supervised; to whom the position reports.
b) Nature and extent of supervision given and received
c) Disclaimer statement
For example: "This job description is not all inclusive and may include other duties as assigned".

Here are other job description principals:
a) Be brief and clear
b) Use present tense
c) Begin each Duty and Responsibility with an action verb

It is my recommendation the job description be authored by the hiring manager and incumbent. If it is written by someone else, such as a human resource representative, it is essential that line management review and approve the job description

> *Paullin's Point—Include key deliverables to be completed in the first twelve months such as reports to be completed, projects to be managed and people to be recruited. Communicate these to candidates along with the job description.*

Here is a job description example:

Director of Finance

JOB SUMMARY

Reporting to the Vice President and Controller, leads the Finance team and advises the Business Units on all finance related matters. Responsibilities include leading all financial planning processes, directing and coordinating the monthly closing process and related variance analyses, providing insightful, value added counsel to the Business Unit leadership teams, developing improved effectiveness analyses and ensuring proper internal controls are in place to safeguard company assets.

PRINCIPAL DUTIES AND RESPONSIBILITIES

Leads the development of the Long Range Plan, Annual Operating Plan, and all related forecasts. Presents each quarter.

Writes plans for risk balance and aligns plans with other cross functional teams.

Defines business exposure areas, researches and validates issues, and provides action plans to mitigate exposure areas to President bi-annually.

Prepares monthly closing and related monthly reporting for executive committee.

Develops, implements, and maintains all general accounting systems to accurately reflect the financial results of all activities. Reports due quarterly to CFO and CEO.

Provides quarterly standardized analyses and explanations of variances from plan, forecast and prior year for the P&L and Balance Sheet. Reports to CFO for operations review.

Works closely with the Director of Operations Finance to ensure closing calendars and reporting and analyses meet the Business Unit's needs.

Effectively interacts as a member of the Senior Business Unit Leadership team by providing sound financial counsel and overall business perspective and insight.

Develops and maintains accurate, timely and relevant data collection systems and procedures to support fact based decision making and analyzes spending effectiveness.

Installs proper controls to safeguard the company's assets.

Reviews and responds in writing to all accounting and control deficiencies identified in audit reviews and ensures timely resolution.

Assists the Business Units in assessing the viability of new products/ventures by providing financial analyses, models and related analyses to ensure Sr. Management clearly understands the risk profile of the product/venture.

Provides ongoing training sessions to improve the understanding of financial analytics across the organization.

Coaches and develops staff by providing training and candid feedback. Conducts annual talent reviews and succession planning processes.

PREFERED EXPERIENCE AND SKILLS
Bachelors Degree in Accounting or Finance, CPA and MBA preferred.

10+ years of experience in leadership roles with full P&L and Balance Sheet accountability.

Strong financial modeling skills. Due diligence experience a plus.

Experience in business process redesign initiatives. Experience with ERP systems a plus, with JDE preferred.

Strong analytical and project management skills

Excellent written and verbal communication skills.

Ability to move comfortably from a Sr. Mgmt to accounting clerk audience.

Strong coaching skills and demonstrated ability to develop staff and promote teamwork and cross-functional projects.

REPORTING RELATIONSHIP
Reports to the Vice President and Controller

DISCLAIMER
This job description is not all inclusive and may include other duties as assigned.

Summary

An up-to-date and current job description is the important starting point of your hiring system. It is also the roadmap necessary for hiring the best. When you hire the best, you will improve company profits and you will create a more positive employee culture. When you do this, you will become a star in the eyes of the leaders you work with.

Your Hiring Firing Experts Notes:

12

Build a Beautiful Applicant Pool

Swimming or Drowning in the Applicant Pool

Recruiting aimed at getting a good applicant pool gives you the option of selecting from the best and sets-up the interviewing process for selecting a championship hire.

Paullin's Point—You can only hire to the depth of your applicant pool.

In recruiting you must set standards to weed out undesirables (**see Resume and TeleScreen Chapters 19 and 20**), but not set standards that will weed out people with superstar potential. The number one example of this is seen by the managers whose objective is to always hire the experienced. Experience can be excellent data, but measure it wisely so that you do not hire someone else's problem. The facts are that some people with ten years experience have one year of experience ten times over. Another applicant may have one year experience, but because of talent and development may be at the five year level. A person with self-motivation and a high ability to learn may in one year be equal to a ten-year veteran lacking either of these two elements. A ten-year self motivated, experienced veteran is great and will hit the deck running.

Creating a Quality Applicant Pool

There are a number of ways to create a quality pool of applicants. Key ways to do this are through:
- Advertising
- Employment Agencies and Executive Search Firms
- Promoting from within your organization
- Employee Referral Programs
- Networking

We will look at each.

Advertise

Use the job description and creatively design an ad that will attract quality people. The ad should sell quality people on applying and screen out undesirables. One way to do this is to list key objectives and deliverables on which the person will be measured. Use commercial, professional and school alumni internet job posting sites.

> *Paullin's Point—Post the job on your company or commercial website including the major tasks that must be completed during the first twelve months. This may screen out people who are really not interested or are not qualified to do the tasks.*

Employment Agencies and Executive Search Firms

Love Them as Partners or Leave Them

Both employment agencies and executive search firms can be well worth the money you pay them, if they are good. I recommend utilizing these valuable resources and treat the good ones as partners.

The One Rule

A few headhunters will send over a parade of zoo animals and at the end throw in one well dressed, smooth talking orangutan. After the zoo parade the well dressed orangutan looks like a quality person and gets hired.

To stop the zoo parade, advise them they may send you their best applicant and you will judge them by that one candidate. After you see their best, you then will be able to decide if you want to see more from them. If their best is a quality applicant, then I will see more from their company. The logic is that they are getting close to what I want. I also believe that initially they may not have the information to know who is actually the best, but may gain that as they understand my needs.

Understand the difference between employment agencies and executive search firms. Some employment agencies charge around 15% to 25% (per hire) of the first year salary of the individual hired, and this is paid once the candidate is hired. Executive search firms may or may not want expense money up front and charge a higher rate (usually 25% to 35% per hire) of the employee's annual package.

Agencies have people on file, but search firms seek out candidates to fit your specific needs. Executive search firms cost more, do more, and become more important as the level of the job rises. At entry level positions and entry level management positions, agencies make economic sense. At higher executive levels, the talents and results of search firms are excellent investments.

I do not believe you will get the best service or candidate by being cheap. If you screen out the incompetent companies, then both agencies and search firms become time and money savers and excellent tools to help you find quality hires. Be fair to agencies and search firms, give them information, pay them fairly, and you will win in ROI. The good headhunters become my friends.

To Gain Value from Agencies and Search Firms
- Be fair—partner with the good ones
- Pay the appropriate fee on time
- Be cooperative
- Share information
- Thank them

Promote From Within Your Organization

When practical, promote from within your company. You will create a morale booster and a stronger management base. Promotions, where the employees perceive there was no internal search, tend to be a demotivator. Employees should know you first looked within the organization, even when you hire externally. *Post that job!* Employees feel better about management when they are considered for the job, even if not hired, than they do about being totally ignored for the position. Plus, your best hire may reside inside your own company.

Promotion from within usually leads to multiple promotions within the organization. This creates a management team that better understands the total operation of the company and is more loyal and dedicated to the mission. Turnover will drop like winter temperatures in Illinois.

Additionally, promotion from within causes managers to develop backup people to perform their jobs. The employee should understand that if no one else can perform their duties, they are stuck performing them. Tell your manager that **if you cannot be replaced, then you cannot be promoted**. When this management philosophy is known and in place, it helps eliminate the panic problem when key individuals leave.

Paullin's Point — Like banks, Bonnie and Clyde would find it easy to steal employees from companies who always recruit externally. It is difficult to steal good employees from organizations who promote from within, even if more money is offered.

Morale Boosting Promotions From Within

A is promoted and B is promoted to A. C is then promoted to B and D is promoted to C. D is now vacant and may be filled by a new hire. This does not create chaos, but a spirit of team building and each person helps train and support the new employee. This is Paullin's Atomic Rule of Multiple Promotions.

Paullin's Atomic Rule of Multiple Promotions
One promotion can explode and chain react to several promotions boosting morale and company loyalty.

$$A \Rightarrow New\ Position$$
$$B \Rightarrow A$$
$$C \Rightarrow B$$
$$D \Rightarrow C$$
$$External\ Hire \Rightarrow D$$

Promotion from Within $\Rightarrow$ *Team building* $\Rightarrow$ *Morale* $\Rightarrow$ *Loyalty*

***Paullin's Point*—Low productive and negative employees will often leave a "promotion from within company" because they constantly get bypassed.**

Employee Referral Programs

I built a successful telemarketing team with an unprecedented low turnover rate. One reason was having my own telemarketers searching for new applicants. My telemarketers understood the job and what type of person it took to do it successfully. I stole from the criminal "Wanted Dead or Alive…$1,000 Reward" posters. Create your own wanted poster: "A person who meets the following job description…$1,000 reward." Have a little creative sense of humor with this and you will get results at most levels because your employees have networks into other companies like yours. Give your employees a monetary reward if it results in a hire because it is much cheaper than ads and the headhunter fees—and they deserve it.

Paullin's Point—Candidates recommended by employees should still undergo the same interviewing selection process as others before a hiring decision is made.

Networking

Take the time to think of organizations and people you know who can find a key hire:

POP (People Of your Past)...Think about your past business experiences because the key individual may be a player that you already know.

PIB (People In Business)...As a pharmaceutical sales manager, I would call doctors and pharmacists and ask them who their best sales representatives are. When a name kept coming up, I knew I had a winner.

PWE (People Without Experience)...Do not eliminate PWE's. They may not have had direct job-related experience, but when their past experience has indicated they can learn and they are talented and self-motivated, PWE's are like diamonds in the rough. When you find them, they may become some of your best employees. The additional time to train PWE's becomes worthwhile because of reduced turnover and high productivity. Utilizing skilled interviewing techniques, you can find PWE's that will be top employees.

The Competition...A happily employed person may not have a current resume. If you are trying to recruit them out of their current company, simply ask for their old resume and a few notes about what they do on their current job. A high producing employee may often be an attractive candidate and may come on board for the right reasons such as promotional opportunities or better employee culture. As a sales manager, I hired away my competitors' top sales people for three reasons: 1) Their performance predicted that they would be successful for me; 2) They were trained to the industry and had an established client following; and 3) This also demoralized my competition.

> *Paullin's Point—When you know how to do it, there are more pros than cons when hiring people away from other companies.*

Summary

Use your creativity to figure out ways to recruit a quality applicant pool. Methods such as ads, particularly on the internet are fine, but explore the other possibilities for a quality, not quantity, applicant pool. Good employment agencies and executive search firms are worth their fees and provide excellent ROI value. Promotion from within boosts morale. Employee referral programs work because good employees tend to refer good candidates. Networking taps and uncovers people you've known in your past, people who know the industry and people who can learn the job and the business.

Your Hiring Firing Experts Notes:

13

Search Firms Will Work for You and Produce ROI Value

Quick Quiz

Pick the best answer: How can search firms and agencies add value to you and your company?

A) Allow your people to do their jobs—ROI
B) Save countless hours of management time
C) Help keep you legal
D) Increase the quality of the applicant pool
E) All of the above

Answer: E) All of the above

Who's Who and What's What? Contingency and Retained Search Firms

Basically search firms come in two varieties: those that work on contingency fees and those that are retained. Contingency firms get paid by the company when the candidate is hired. Contingency firms usually do not get exclusive contracts and therefore compete with other contingency firms and candidates to make a placement. Retained firms may bill the company a percent of their fee up front and then in phases, for example in thirds with the final payment being made after the candidate is placed. Retained firms typically are given exclusive contracts to select the best candidates in the world for a position. This makes sense because you are paying in phases and want them to give you their maximum effort and attention.

The word Agency usually refers to employment agencies. There are temporary employment agencies, temp-to-hire agencies, and leasing agencies who actually are the employer of record for a professional population and bill out professional staff, literally leasing them, billing them by the hour, or renting them out for a term. As a client, one has to determine the agency's principals of operation and their rules of engagement, and you will understand what each firm does, exactly how they do it, and how the transaction is funded. Now that you know what is what, you can select what best fits your needs.

A "Headhunter" by any Other Name

A headhunter is a professional matchmaker who defines himself or herself in a non-ambiguous fashion. I have heard it all. The professional you interview can be a recruiter, an executive search consultant, employment match consultant, or probably half a dozen flowery monikers— in reality that person is a headhunter.

Great headhunters are your best friends when it comes to getting the best applicant pool. Having a true veteran for a headhunter helps you select the best hire, and this often is the most viable recruitment strategy. The firm that does the most for you in making you successful in your mission is the priority agency to work with.

How to Work With Search Firms

Can the search firm that dictates the search methodology as, "This is the way we do it" and displays an unwillingness to be flexible be of service? That depends upon their expertise and historic track record. Great search agencies are artisans of sorts, and they may well have insights and experience you do not. Don't ask the unreasonable, but do thoroughly define your mission and do tell the search firm what you need that will help you. You're the boss and writing the checks.

If a search firm asks you for an exclusive from the inception of your conversations with them, then beware of the bad wolf. Conversely, if they are doing a specific search for a key individual who exists in a very small population (example CEO), then it might be worth it. To fill your various job openings, you may have to work with a number of search firms simply because some firms are more distinctly competent or are specialists, and may for example, do engineering but not administrative or financial positions.

Define what you consider complete due diligence, and a professional search firm will do it well.

> *Paullin's Point—Ask the search firm to ask the candidate to provide copies of degrees, transcripts, CPA licenses or any relevant documents. As the hiring company, letting the search firm do the leg work and heavy lifting allows for a generally more positive interaction with a candidate but still gets you the hard answers and facts you need.*

Headhunter Acid Tests

Acid test one: If you don't feel the chemistry and enjoy "the moment" or the initial conversation with the headhunter is choppy, contentious or uninformative, then they are more likely going to be a negative experience.

Acid test two: If you enjoy calling your headhunter and consider them a partner, then they are more likely to evolve as your partner in the mission.

Acid Test Three: Does the firm GUARANTEE their work? Terms vary, but for management level personnel, I would press for a 90-day guarantee.

Acid test Four: Trust is a must...well, do you or don't you trust the agency? How has their performance caused you to feel?

Cast Your Bread on the Water and it will Come back 10-Fold

I believe in paying search firms a fair fee and not trying to negotiate too cheap a fee. You will likely get the effort you pay for. Use good judgment in bottom line negotiations. Pay fair and on time, and it will likely pay off in better candidates, saved time, friendships, and ROI.

Summary

Having too many search firms work an assignment is like too many boyfriends or girlfriends...it does not lead to marriage. In fact, my experience has been with contingency search, one is not enough and more than three are too many. They work for you, but it is a two-way street. Having too many firms is not fair to the firms really working for you and will discourage each firm.

Give back to your good search firms, and they will in return work for you harder. Giving back means giving them good, up-to-date, and complete information. Provide a detailed job description, an overview of the corporate culture, details on the hiring manager, and compensation and benefit package information at a minimum.

- A poor search firm means frustration
- A good search firm means good hires and saved time
- A great search firm means a partner helping contribute great hires and ROI

14

Recruiting Interns for Future Leadership

So why are you hiring an intern?
A) For cheap labor
B) For future developmental talent
C) Don't know why

Answer: The value of an intern can be either A) cheap labor or B) future developmental talent but rarely both.

One strategy is to select high caliber undergraduate and MBA students who one day may be key leaders in the company. High caliber individuals can inject innovation and creativity into the company. This is also an excellent way to increase the diversity of the company's talent pool.

Where to Begin
Interns are key to recruitment of fulltime talent because the intern and the company have dated before getting married—or have tried each other out.

Successful intern programs need the endorsement and support of senior management. This is so for continuous improvement of the program, meaningful job assignments, and the cultivation of ongoing relationships with the targeted universities.

The first step in having a successful intern program is to identify meaningful assignments commensurate with the level and caliber of intern you are planning to recruit. The job description along with job objectives that are accountable and measurable need to be created. This should be done by the position manager.

The Candidate Profile needs to be determined. The generalities of the profile should be agreed upon by all hiring managers.

University relations are important. It is recommended targeting schools and using alumni employees as university "emissaries." Also, former interns who are alumni are excellent company representatives.

The Recruiting Process

Recruiting occurs typically in the fall or early winter of each year. On-campus presentations and interviews are completed in September—November followed with final candidate interviews in December—February.

Each intern position needs a job description upon which Predictors are identified and Predictor questions are written. Since work experience is not as extensive as that of more senior candidates, Predictors such as Analytical Skills, Attendance and Punctuality, Communication Skills—oral and written, Planning, Organizing and Time Management, Responsiveness and Work Ethics need to be probed.

It could be argued that the intern position is so important for future leadership positions that Judgment, Self Motivation, Integrity, Interpersonal Skills, Creativity, and the Ability to Understand and Learn are also important Predictors.

The resume review is the same as with any position. Select your A, B, and C resumes and go after the A's as described in the ABC's of Time Management in **Chapter 19**.

The campus interview takes the place of the TeleScreen and one-on-one interview. Beyond this, the interview sequence should be the same as outlined in **Chapter 10**, e.g., references, team interviews, team evaluation, etc.

Preparing for Your Intern

With such a short time frame that the intern works, proper planning for the intern is key to maximizing his or her time in position. Develop a pre-arrival checklist involving work space, telephone, PC, mail, and supplies, etc.

On-Boarding

The on-boarding of the intern is similar to the on-boarding of full time hires. Follow the steps and use the information in **Chapter 28**, Bringing the New Hire On-Board. This will help ensure your intern's positive experience.

The On-the-Job Experience

Providing the job description, measurable goals, and objectives are essential for a meaningful intern assignment.

The intern should experience the company's culture. This can be gained through inclusion in departmental meetings, company communication sessions, appropriate classroom training, extra-curricular outings, and other company events.

When the intern is on board, a mentor might be assigned. Also part of the experience may be to set up meetings with key executives in the department and across other departments, including the CEO.

Regular performance feedback should be given to the intern along with a formal performance appraisal at the end of the internship.

The intern should also be given the opportunity to have an exit interview so the company can learn what's good and what may need to change or be improved about the overall experience and the intern program.

Summary

A good intern experience will pay dividends back on campus through positive company publicity and good will conveyed by the intern to other students. Conversely, the opposite holds true if the intern's experience is not so good.

The key is to be well prepared for the intern at every stage: pre-interview campus visits; campus and site interviews; the intern period; and with performance feedback and the exit. The objective is to select the best talent who can become future leaders in the company.

Your Hiring Firing Experts Notes:

15

How to Predict Future Job Performance

Predict the Future and Be a Fortune Teller

> *Paullin's Point—Past job history is the best Predictor of today's and tomorrow's job performance.*

How to Pick the Best Person: Past Job History Predicts Today's and Future Job Performance

How do you really know for sure how the candidate will perform for you on the job? The only sure thing that I know is there is no way to know for sure! WAIT...before you throw this book away, I can provide you with the best Predictor of how the candidate will perform for you on your particular job even if he or she has never held a similar position.

Read the Tea Leaves and Become a Fortune Teller

How is a professional athlete paid? How is a CEO hired? How do they pick horses to win races? All are decisions based on their history of past job performances. How do you best predict how the candidate will perform on your job? You can accurately predict how the candidate will perform on your particular job even if they have never held that position in a past company.

Read the History of Job Performance

Master this concept then you will be able to *predict* with a high degree of accuracy if the candidate will:

Get along with fellow employees and even customers

(Team player vs. a person with a "me" attitude)

Work when you are not there to supervise

(When nobody is there watching, will the self-starting salesperson actually get out of bed before the crack of noon?)

Make more good business decisions or more bad business decisions

(Simply put, without good decisions, the company fails!)

Be able to learn on the job

(A quick study on the job can catch up with experienced people—if they can't learn on the job, they fail)

Be loyal to the company and manager

(No knives in your back or your company's)

Be able to handle stress and pressure

(Whiners and Victims need not apply)

Define what you need on the job and then learn the candidate's job history, and you can predict how the candidate will perform on the job today, tomorrow and in the future.

I am often asked the question: can history predict the future of boyfriends, girlfriends, husbands, wives, kids, bosses, and dogs. Yes, it predicts for all.

Here are some fun projects. Write the job descriptions for: A fun boyfriend/girlfriend and a future husband/wife; a pet dog and guard dog; or a loyal friend and fun friend.

Look at their past history to see how successful they will be in the job description you've written and how successful they will be in their future possibilities.

Past job history of performance is the best Predictor of future job performance and the most current history is the very best Predictor of today's and tomorrow's performance. My mother told my girlfriend that I left my socks on the floor when I was a kid, and I always talked to strangers. My girlfriend told my mom I still believe the floor to be my sock drawer, and I've never met a stranger I didn't like.

When you hire a person, what you see in their history is what you will get on your job in today's and tomorrow's performance.

> ## *Paullin's Point—You may think that you can change a person but, stop before you get shortchanged.*

Think how difficult it is for you to change. You will smile and understand that what they did in the past is what they will do in the future. Ask the wardens of prisons how many bad guys change and become good guys. Ask women if men can be changed before you marry a man that you will have to change. Think about the odds of changing the person. Hire or marry the winner and let some other sad manager or spouse try to change the loser into a winner.

Facts:
- Banks make loans primarily based on past credit history;

- NFL football players are drafted and paid based on their past college gridiron history

- Colleges look at high school grades and SAT scores for admittance

- Sales reps are hired based on their history of past sales records

- CEO's are hired based on their past company's performance history.

My banker tells me that I have opened twenty-seven new checking accounts in the past fifteen years. I get in too much of a hurry and so I fail to record checks. I don't have time to actually subtract the amount from the balance and so reconciliation with the monthly bank statement is certainly something that can wait until the next century. After a few months of this, I absolutely have no idea of how much money is in the account. My solution is not to work it out, but rather to open a new account, along with a new resolution to keep the balance. Incidentally, I am great at balancing the new account for about two months and then I revert back to my past performance. After six months of no records, I open a new account and eventually close the old one. Past performance will predict future performance!

So here are some past performance facts:
• If a person was late to work on their last job, then they will likely be late on your Job;

• If a person speaks poorly about his past bosses and companies, then he will probably be a negative mouth about you and your company;

• If a person has a good track record of punctuality and attendance on their last job, then you can bet on them being at their desk when the bell rings at your place;

• If a person speaks positively about their former managers and fellow employees, then you are going to have a loyal team player;

• If a person is the number one salesperson for XYZ Company, they likely will be a competitor for number one at your company; and if they are an average salesperson at XYZ Company, then you will likely get an average performer at your company.

Predictors are Key to Superior Interview Questions and Superior Questions are Based on the Job Description
If past job history of performance is the best Predictor of how the candidate will perform in your job, then when designing interview questions, you must learn how to write questions which tell you how the candidate performed in the past. The answers to those questions will indicate how they will perform in your job. Later in this book, you will learn how to evaluate answers so that you will be able to quantitatively grade the candidate by numbers ranging from one to five, indicating poor to superior performance.

So, let's review some good questions to ask and not ask:

Do ask questions that give you specific data on past performance:

Tell me about your biggest business decision at ABC Corporation.

Do ask follow-up questions to give you more data and better data to make your hiring decision:

What were the results of that decision at ABC? What did your boss say?

Would you use your managers at ABC and XYZ Companies as references?

If not, why not?

If Yes, their names? Phone numbers?

Why will they say you left?

When we call them, what will they tell us your strengths are?

What will they say they asked you to improve on?

What will they verify your ending salary was?

Do ask:

At XYZ how often did you take work home in the evenings? Give me a couple of specific examples.

Do ask:

Were you ever promoted in your five years at XYZ?

Do not ask:

Where do you want to be in five years?

I think the point is made by the following:

Don't ask theoretical or hypothetical questions like—

Will you work extra evenings to accomplish a project? (Everyone will say yes.)

Paullin's Point—Theoretical and hypothetical questions give you beautiful theoretical and hypothetical answers that make-up a comfortable conversation. But these leave you with weak decision making data for predicting success.

Don't gamble. Design *specific* questions that deal with past performance and you will have a good idea of what you are hiring.

You will find over 300 Predictor Interviewing questions in Chapter 29.

16

Performance Predictors

*Hire Championship Performers
For Raises, Praises, Promotions,
and Fat Profits*

> **Paullin's Point—Managers who hire superstars get superstar productivity, get promoted, and create fat profits.**

Predictors for Designing Interview Questions and Making Best Hires

To be an effective interviewer, you must understand the Predictors of the job performance you desire. The key Predictors that *Hiring Firing Experts* define from the job descriptions are easy to understand and will save you time, money, and frustration.

Predictors are Job Performance Traits that Predict Job Performance

Before you can write your Predictor interview questions, you must know exactly what Predictors are needed for the position. What you need to know is found in the well-written job description. Employees who have held the position or managed the position can also be valuable resources in ascertaining the essential Predictors the candidate must have to be capable of performing the job.

> *Hiring Firing Experts defines Predictors as necessary traits of job performance on which a conclusion for making the best hire can be based.*

Select the Predictors that are the most important to the job. To help you with Predictors for a sales job, here are some examples:

SS & PP- Selling Skills & Persuasive Power
CO- Communication Skills—Oral
POT- Planning, Organization & Time Management
IC- Innovative/Creative Solutions
T- Tenacity
J- Judgment
WE- Work ethics
SM- Self Motivation
R- Responsiveness
MS&L- Management Skills & Leadership

Knowing how applicants score on the Predictors allows an evidence based team evaluation that helps hire the best candidate.

After you have analyzed your job description and interviewed employees that have held or managed the position, then select the Predictors that are the most important to the job.

The Magic Number

Usually you will develop questions designed from eight to twelve Predictors from the job description. Select only your key Predictors. More than twelve Predictors become difficult to judge and lessen the probability of hiring the best. Prioritize your key Predictors and reduce them to a manageable number that will allow the best hiring.

You may wish to take the final Predictors you've selected and prioritize that list even further to come up with the top five or so that are most critical to the job. In the sales rep example above you would have ten Predictors, but the top five would be the most critical Predictors.

Major Predictors Common to Many Positions

ANL- Analytical skills

AP- Attendance and punctuality

AUL- Ability to understand and learn (Quick study—learn fast)

CO- Communication Skills—Oral (Communication is key to understanding and persuasiveness)

CS- Computer Skills

CW- Communication Skills—Written (Reports, emails, proposals etc.)

E- Estimating

F- Firing

FLX- Flexibility (Adaptability to change)

H- Hiring

IC- Innovative/Creative solutions

INT- Integrity and truthfulness

IPS- Interpersonal skills (Ability to get along with customers and fellow employees)

J- Judgment (If an executive or manager makes poor decisions, he and his company are in trouble; conversely, a manager making good decisions spells success; low judgment is a knockout Predictor for most executive positions)

L- Loyalty (Does my back have a knife in it or a "pat" on it?)

MS&L- Management Skills & Leadership (Ability to persuade, lead others and manage)

POT- Planning, Organization & Time Management (Without POT, follow-up, scheduling, estimating time, setting deadlines, etc are in jeopardy)

PS- Platform Skills (Ability to do public speaking and facilitate groups and meetings)

R- Responsiveness (Willingness to go the extra mile for customers and clients)

R&D- Risk-Taking & Decisiveness (R&D is the propensity for a person to take risks and make decisions; low R&D is also a knockout for most executive positions)

SC- Self Confidence (For leadership, sales and police officers)

SCHD- Scheduling projects (Critical for project or product managers)

SD- Self-development (Self-initiated activities such as taking courses, reading books and engaging in extra work activities for career development)

SM- Self-motivation (Demonstrates pride and self-initiation; Does job for the sake of doing it right; very important for jobs requiring self-starters, and people who work virtually. Example: field sales people, and if it is not there, a KO for sales people)

SS&PP- Selling Skills and Persuasive Power

ST- Stress tolerance

SWS- Software Skills

T- Tenacity (Persistence and diligence; sticks with job despite adversity)

TM- Time management (see POT)

TP- Technical proficiency (Used to assess computer skills, engineering skills, etc)

WE- Work ethics (Adheres to rules and standards of conduct; demonstrates trust in putting in a full day's work for a full day's pay)

Predictor Knockouts or KO's

There are certain key Predictors that are so critical that if candidates score low on that Predictor, they are eliminated no matter their score on the other Predictors. Watch for KO Predictors in your job description.

Examples of KO Predictors Related to Specific Areas:

J—Judgment for key executives

SM—Self Motivation for any job that requires a self-starter, like field sales reps

INT—Integrity for accounting people

IPS—Interpersonal Skills for customer service people

IC—Innovation and Creativity for advertising copywriters

CS—Computer Skills for the IT department

AUL—Ability to Understand & Learn for employees who must learn on the job

It is up to the interviewing team or hiring manager to define if there are any KO Predictors.

Predictors represent key traits of the candidate's past job history that will help predict success or failure in the position. Past job history predicts today's, tomorrow's and next year's job performance. The Predictors you select relating to the job description allow you to quantitatively predict the applicant's likely performance on that job. Predictors are keys to hiring the best.

It is critical to develop the best questions from the correctly defined Predictors from the job description. This invested time will allow you to analytically evaluate past job performance to predict which candidate will perform the best on your job today, tomorrow and next year and make you a fortuneteller…or a fortune.

Your Hiring Firing Experts Notes:

17

Writing Predictor Questions to Predict Success

> *It is better to ask ten times than to go astray once.—Yiddish proverb*

In the last chapter, Hiring Firing Experts defined Predictors as the necessary traits of job performance on which a conclusion for making the best hire can be based.

The next step is to write specific questions to determine the applicant's past history on the particular job Predictor. Remember, the questions must be all job related to stay away from prejudicial legal problems.

This chapter will be devoted to giving you some examples of Predictor questions. The examples will help you write your own performance or Predictor questions. It is important to note that a Predictor question may lead to an answer that will give data on other Predictors. Below are some Predictor questions designed to give you job history performance which will predict future performance on that specific element of the job.

In order to give you a start on preparing your interview, I have listed sample questions and follow-up questions for *some* of the **Predictors** discussed in **Chapter 16**. *Over 300 questions are listed is in Chapter 29.*

Additionally you will come up with questions of your own.

AP- Attendance and Punctuality

You stated that you would use your manager, Ms. Jones, as a reference. When we call her, how many times will she tell us you were late last year?...days that you were absent last year?

Tell me how many days you missed or were late at XYZ in the last two years?

What did your performance appraisal say about your punctuality and attendance?

AUL- Ability to Understand and Learn

What was your GPA in high school? In College?

What grade did you receive in your computer course?

How many times did it take you to pass your CPA exam?

How many times did it take to pass the bar exam?

Tell me how you did in learning on the job?

How did you learn Microsoft Suite?

How did you develop your IT skills?

How did you learn your new company's system?

Where did you rank in your class on_____?

CO- Communication Skills—Oral (One hour of interviewing should give you the data to evaluate oral communications.)

In your jobs did you ever have the opportunity to make an oral presentation to a group? Follow-up...How did you do and what were the results?

Tell me about some large groups you have spoken to? Results?

Are you a member of Toastmasters or any other speaking group?

Tell me about an oral report that you made at ABC? How was it received?

CW- Communication Skills—Written

Tell me about a written report that you made at ABC? How was it received?

What RFP's have you written? What were the results?

What did your manager say about your written report?

What type of business plans have you written? Proposals? RFP's?

What grades will your transcript show that you received in your English courses?...Term paper?

Tell me about the most important business document that you have written.

Tell me about any instructional or technical manuals that you have written.

FLX- Flexibility—Adaptability to Change

Tell me about a time at ABC when you had a plan in which you had to alter course. What did you do? What did you think?

When they changed the computer system at ABC, how did you feel? What did you do?

When they announced the new manager, how did you feel? How did you react?

IC- Innovative and Creative solutions

What things are they doing differently at XYZ Company because of you?

Did you cause any changes at CBS?

What did you introduce to XYZ?

HIR- Hiring

Tell me about the last two hires that you made? Are they still with the company? Why or why not? If they are still with the company, how are they doing?

Tell me about any people you have hired who have been promoted?

How do you go about your hiring process?

Give me an example of a favorite interview question you ask.

What information are you trying to find?

How many people do you manage?

What positions were you responsible for filling?

How did your hires do?

INT- Integrity and Truthfulness

Integrity and truthfulness are very difficult to come up with specific questions to measure. A liar will probably tell you he does not lie, and a "truther" will tell you that, yes, he has lied in his lifetime. **Truthfulness and integrity are usually best checked during referencing.** It is important to understand that I don't really ask questions on telling the truth, but I almost always catch liars or persons with low integrity stumbling and making mistakes during the regular interview process. Follow-up questions will trip up the smooth talking con artist.

Examples:

You said Mr. Jones was your manager at XYZ and that we could use him as a reference. When we call him, why will he say you left?

Would you send me a copy of your performance appraisal... transcript?

I put the burden on the candidate. Ask them to send you a copy of their transcript. If for any reason they do not do this, it tells you about how they will perform for you. They may not have the grades they told you or the degree or it tells you that their follow-up is bad.

> *A comprehensive list of Predictors and questions are in* *Chapter 29.*

18

Your Time Saving Predictor Interview Guide

Building Predictor Interview Guides
Which are Easy to Use and Ensure you Hire the Best

You can go to the Game

Decision: Tiger's Baseball Game with Son or Compose Seven Interviews

As a young sales manager, I was taught to write out custom interviews on a blank pad for each applicant. It took one hour per applicant! I noticed that many of my interview questions were the same, covering the same job description and were designed to give me the same information for making my hiring decision. Writing seven custom interview forms from candidate's resumes would take approximately seven hours.

This would mean telling my nine-year-old son, "No going to the Detroit Tigers game, as promised, because Daddy has to spend Sunday writing out his interviews for Monday." Ouch—on being nominated for the Dad of the Year Award!! Dad came up with a game saving play. I could write one really great interview based on job description questions and make seven copies. I could then use each candidate's resume to make questions candidate specific. Example: Tell me about the sales awards and bonuses you received at ABC? From the resume, just put the name of the company in the blank and it becomes candidate specific.

I wrote the questions in one hour and made seven copies of what would become my World Famous Time Saving Signature **Predictor Interview Guide**. "Son, lets go watch the Detroit Tigers beat the New York Yankees. Son, Dad just invented what will become the world renowned Predictor Interview Guide that will allow thousands of fathers to have the time to take their sons to ball games." My son was impressed by his father's grandiose, unsubstantiated world claim and shared his father's world-renowned claim in show-and-tell class the next day. The teacher called me the next day and explained the horrors of exaggerating to kids.

The Results

I hired three rookies of the year for a Fortune 500 pharmaceutical company and all were from my time saving Predictor Interview Guide. My hiring results were so astounding, I got promoted, and companies are now paying me to use my Predictor Interview Guides. I also invented Guides for Phone Screens and Reference Checks. These Predictor Interview Guides and my time saving ideas would become the foundation for ways to improve hiring and firing. In turn, this would allow fathers and mothers to have time to have fun with their kids, while basing their careers on the great hires they would make (and by the way, while receiving praises and raises).

Cakes Not Interviews Should Be Made From Scratch

My son learned that copying can be good. That cakes, not interviews, should be made from scratch and the baseball game story would someday become part of my book about hiring the best. Because of the seven copied Predictor Interview Guides, my son and I were able to have baseball, hotdogs, and apple-pie. And by copying the Predictor Interview Guides, all candidates were treated consistently and this reduced worry over lawsuits.

Writing the Predictor Interview Guide

The value of a Predictor Interview Guide will become evident the first time you use it. **See Chapter 30 for an example Predictor Interview Guide.** The applicant will sense how prepared you are and most of all, it will give you confidence that you are in control. The interview guide is not meant to be read or to kill the spontaneity of additional questions. Adding your spontaneous questions and follow-up questions are an essential part of the actual interviewing process. (Just remember EEOC compliance, and treat everybody the same.)

The part managers tend to hate is writing out the interview questions. The nice thing is with the Predictor Interview Guide, once it is written it can be used on all candidates.

Use the Job Description

Utilizing the job description, select the important Predictors that you need data on in order to make a good hiring decision. As a general rule, remember to select only eight to twelve Predictors. Once you go over twelve it becomes less measurable and less valuable for decision-making purposes. You only need the key priority Predictors.

Examples:

Predictor: AUL (Ability to Understand and Learn)

Questions: What was your grade point at the University of Chicago?
What was your GPA in the MBA program at Notre Dame?
How did you learn to operate computers at Northland Corporation?
How many times did you take the CPA exam before passing?

Predictor: SM (Self Motivation)

Questions: What did you like about your job at ABC?
Have you ever taken work home in the evening? Why?
Why did you apply for this position?
Why did you leave ABC?
What promotions did you get at ABC?
What salary increases did you get at ABC? How often (time wise), how much and why?
When did you know that you wanted to be an accountant?
Why did you go to engineering school?

Predictor: POT (Planning, Organization and Time Management)

Questions: How, exactly did you start your business day at ABC?
You prepared the budget at Northland—what were the results of that budget?
What did your manager, Mr. Jones, say about that budget?
You had a lot of areas (things) that you were responsible for at XYZ. How did you keep the projects going without dropping the ball?

Predictor: SS (Selling Skills)

Questions: How many people were in your sales force at ABC Pharmaceuticals? Where did you rank in the sales force?
Did you win any awards in your last jobs that you would like to tell me about?

How often and how much of a bonus did you receive? How did that compare to other sales representatives?

What rating did you receive on your performance appraisal for sales?

After you have written down your selected Predictors and questions, it is simply a matter of placing them in the Predictor Interview Guide where you want them. It is probably best not to group all of the same Predictor questions in sequence. Instead, place them throughout the guide and use them with different jobs that the candidate has held.

You are now armed with the basic structure on how to set up a specific "past job history predicts future job performance" Predictor Interview Guide. Simply define the Predictors that you need from the job description and write out your questions. To help you in learning how to write questions, **Chapters 29 and 30** provide key Predictors and written example interview questions and an example of a Predictor Interview Guide.

Space is Necessary

When designing your Predictor Interview Guide, remember to leave space between questions to write notes on the candidate's answers and space to interject additional spontaneous questions geared to each specific candidate. Once you learn how to use your Predictor Interview Guide, it will save you hours of time, frustration, and you will always be professionally prepared.

Just Say No to Unneeded Questions

You should not use every question in your Predictor Interview Guide for many reasons. By design, you may have put more questions than you need and you may always think of questions to ask during the interview. Just scratch out the question you don't want and write in the question that you feel is better.

> *Paullin's Point—Having your Predictor Interview Guide as a template on your computer makes it easy to keep improving the guide by deleting and adding questions.*

Predictor Interview Guides vs. Custom Made Guides

Very few managers have the time to write a Predictor Interview Guide from scratch for each applicant, and I do not recommend doing this. It takes about one hour to write a Predictor Interview Guide that covers the scope of twelve Predictors, but once prepared, it takes only seconds to retrieve the template for use again. Once I wrote my first Predictor Interview Guide, I never again went back to writing new interviews from scratch for each candidate.

Three Heads Are Better Than One

The initial interviewing process should be the responsibility of the hiring manager, but you will get much better hires and reduce turnover if you have other managers also interview the candidates. Ideally, three managers should interview each candidate separately. My rule is no more than three managers interviewing and no less than two. The candidate should visit and be introduced to the other players to make the best impression and get people involved. More than three managers actually interviewing tends to confuse the process, turn the applicant off, and demonstrate indecisive management to the applicant.

The ABC's of Predictor Interview Guides

I recommend selecting questions for three interviewers (Guides A, B, & C) and placing the Predictor questions in the three different guides. These three guides are given to the three interviewing managers and are used for all candidates. This allows three managers to have different sets of prepared and coordinated Predictor questions over the selected job. The first manager uses guide A, second guide B, and the third Guide C. Each manager does not need three questions per Predictor except on the key Predictors. Manager A may have two questions on the Predictor AUL (Ability to Understand and Learn); Manager B, only one question; and Manager C may not have any questions at all on this Predictor. Design the questions and guides to cover each Predictor for data. It is okay for managers to ask a few of the exact same questions. This is good to test the integrity of the candidate, because the follow-up questions will be different by the managers and tend to bring out the entire story and find any discrepancies if they exist.

> *Paullin's Point—Let good judgment be the deciding factor on selecting and distributing the questions in the ABC guides.*

After each interview, each manager immediately and individually scores the candidate. Then as soon as possible, the managers meet to discuss evaluation scores and make a decision on the candidates. The Predictor Interview Guides are then collected and kept as documentation in the event of future justification or a legal suit.

Knock Out Candidates

A Predictor may be so essential to the job as to KO (knock out) the candidate who is lacking in that Predictor (an example would be **Judgment** for leadership positions). All three managers' guides should have questions on KO Predictors for leadership positions.

The important thing to make sure when designing the three Predictor Interview Guides is that the KO Predictors you have selected are covered by at least two if not all three Interview Guides.

The Big Ten Purposes of the Predictor Interview Guide

1. Ready preparedness for the Interview based on the job description
2. Candidate has a positive impression of you and the company
3. Save hours of time and frustration by not writing custom interviews
4. Help stay within legal guidelines- applicants are treated equally by the same standards
5. Provide an evaluation score for comparing and decision making
6. Interviewing by teams (ABC guides or 3 guides for 3 interviewers) for less turnover
7. Provide documentation in case of challenges or discrimination claims avoiding lawsuits
8. Make the best hire by hiring people you should (avoid false negatives)
9. Avoid hiring the wrong people (avoid false positives)
10. Better interviewing and better evaluation for the best hires and better profits

EEOC and the Legal Eagles
This book is not a substitute for consulting with attorneys. They are the source for sound legal advice. This book steers you toward legal compliance and the Predictor Interview Guide is in concert with the idea that all candidates must be treated similarly. That is the law. The Predictor Interview Guide uses an evaluation system solely based on the job description. It helps you treat all people equally and provides documentation in the event of questions or legal challenges.

Go to **Chapter 30** for Predictor Interview Guide guidelines, instructions and example.

Your Hiring Firing Experts Notes:

19

Resume Screaming or Screening

The truth is a resume, when read properly, is full of good and bad scenes and is a document that provides data to help weed out even the slickest phony.

Resume Screen First

It makes sense to do the resume screen before a TeleScreen from a time management standpoint. If you have fifty-plus applicants, it will take ten minutes per applicant to screen them by phone. Some resumes you will screen out in a matter of seconds.

The other nice thing about resume screening first is it really cuts down on those awkward number of times that you have to tell the candidate that you will not be granting them an actual interview.

> *and make three distinct A,B,C piles. The "A" group becomes applicants that you will take to the next step. The "B" group represents borderline applicants. After further study, then you will put them in the A group or C group. The "C" group does not qualify for the next step and will not receive further consideration.*

By using the "ABC" resume piles, you can actually compare candidates and prioritize applicants. By TeleScreening your "A" pile, you can determine how well the candidates do in oral communication skills, interpersonal skills and other Predictors and their real motivational level for your job and company.

> *Paullin's Point—As a general rule: resume screen, prioritize into "A," "B," and "C" piles, then TeleScreen only the "A" pile.*

Resumes have two primary benefits: They can be used as K.O. (Knock Out) screening tools, and they can provide the basic data for writing your Predictor Interview Guide on the candidate.

Screen for Your Job Needs

Required Background

Example: Must have CPA license

Must be an R.N.

Must be a licensed civil engineer

Must have a drivers license

(If it is required, you must be able to prove it is essential to job performance.)

Preferred Background

Example: Education-prefer college degree or MBA

Prefer SPC certification

Prefer experience with Apple PC's

Check Job History

 Job hopper or job stability

 Smooth transition between jobs or time gaps between jobs.

 Promotions

 Applicable job experience

 History of successful progression

Check Performance History

 What were their Specific achievements?

Do detective work

 Example: Have they worked for people you know who could give you insights?

 Did they leave their former job for the right or wrong reasons?

Check Salary History

 Are they in or out of your range…may be big time saver—often not on resume, however.

Lie-abilities, Rabbits and Carrots

To further prove my point that resumes do have "Lie-abilities", during the reference check, you will clearly uncover the smooth talkers who lie on both the resume and the interview. You will also decrease your "Rabbit Turnover" if you do not hire job hoppers. These "Rabbits" don't get the carrots (promotions and raises) and their job hopping is evident from the time sequence in their job history on the resume. Finally, do not be overly impressed by a good-looking resume, because a professional may have prepared it.

> ### *Paullin's Point—Look at the player, not the uniform. Look at the data, not the paper. Skilled resume understanding tells you what a resume says and does not say… and this says a lot.*

Read the "Feathers"

 Examples: (Think of "Feathers" as fluff or they are short on the specifics.)

 No dates by jobs or skipped periods of time.

 Instead of specific achievements and results, it contains job descriptions

 No record of promotions or advancement

Only one page usually means not many achievements, unless they are an entry-level person with little job experience.

I also take exception with the opinion that says do not hire a person with a multi—page resume. If the multi-page resume contains successful experience and solid results, then you may have a proud, self-motivated achiever. If the resume is too long and contains a lot of fluff about belonging to the ping-pong club (unless the position is for the ping-pong team), then it indicates poor judgment. You are judging their judgment.

See the Movie and Give Thumbs Up or Thumbs Down

In summary, a resume is like a movie trailer, which shows only the good scenes. Not until you see the movie, or in this case learn to read the resume, will the bad scenes or hidden liabilities become apparent.

20

The Ten-Minute TeleScreen That Works

> *Reach-out, touch someone and let your fingers do the walking.—*
> *Old Ma Bell and her ad agents*

I like ad agencies because they understand selling the sizzle and not the steak. In other words, the benefits instead of the features. The phone can let you reach out and touch your applicants and saves everybody lots of walking time. Time is money, and it is really wasted on interviewing a clearly unacceptable candidate. My ten-minute TeleScreen will eliminate hours of time interviewing unqualified people and that is "time money."

It is federal law that all parts of the selection system must be legal and not discriminatory. There will be few problems if you are following my gospel and write your TeleScreen with only questions that are job related. It's that easy—**JOB RELATED.** If it is not job related— leave it out! To keep you legal and fair, the TeleScreen should be written out so that all people screened will have the same opportunity. If the TeleScreen is written, then this task can be delegated to a trained individual to save the manager even more "time money."

The main purpose of a TeleScreen is to eliminate candidates for interviewing. But, it can also be used to prioritize the candidates that seem best and that you want to see first. This may get that champion hire in first, before another employer beats you to the candidate.

STEP ONE:

The first step in the TeleScreen is to give the candidate a brief, but fair, job description. This means telling them what the job is, including the positives and negatives. By giving the candidates this information, this is their opportunity to decide whether or not they want to stay in the interview process or to drop out now.

STEP TWO:

After giving them the brief job description, it is imperative that you then ask if this sounds like a job they would be interested in doing. Listen to what they say, how they say it and listen to what they "do not" say. Listen also for "feathers." In other words listen to their specifics or lack of specifics; their enthusiasm or lack of enthusiasm; their passion and emotion or lack of passion and emotion.

Weekend Work

I once solved a client's high turnover by simply finding out the people hired were never told that the employees had to work on Saturdays. Some who were hired did not want to work on Saturdays and quit. When applicants are told the "Saturdays" of the job, a few will drop out voluntarily and the ones with real interest will stay. Bringing out the job negatives saves you time, and you will be left with a better chance of filling the position with a person who will stay with the job.

STEP THREE:

After the applicant has heard the job description and has made the decision to continue in the interviewing process, begin asking the TeleScreen questions. The TeleScreen questions will be similar to the questions that you will be asking during a regular interview. (Yes, you read it right! You can actually take questions from your regular interview to make up your TeleScreen, which makes it easier.)

Go to **Chapter 30** for TeleScreen guidelines, instructions, and example.

TeleScreen Tip—Go have Coffee

To avoid the awkward moment of telling the candidate that you do not want to see them for an actual interview remember the following line: *"We will be talking with several other applicants before selecting who we will be bringing in for personal interviews. If you do not hear from us by* _____ *(give a date no longer than 3-5 days from this interview), that means you probably will not. Thank you for talking with me today. Goodbye. "* This is a nice and more comfortable way to let the applicant down without hard-core rejection.

If you tell them "no" on the spot, they may ask you why; you are then forced to defend, and the confrontation begins. If you want to be brutally honest, put on your boxing gloves and defend yourself in the ring and possibly in court. It is your decision to defend and invite confrontation or go have a cup of coffee. I prefer Starbucks to defending.

Your Hiring Firing Experts Notes:

21

You're the Commander of the Interview

Early Birds Don't Get the Worm

After you've prioritized your "A" pile of resumes and did your TeleScreens, you are ready to start your interviews. **It is important to know that managers tend to not hire the first people interviewed. Managers tend to hire the later candidates who are freshest in their memory.** *To avoid this memory problem, compare your notes daily and rate the candidates in order. When you do this, you may wish to bring the best early candidate back!*

Paullin's Point—Are you thinking about what you can't ask and all the rules? You only need to focus on the one thing you can ask about...the job description and this is a key step in successfully controlling the interview.

Controlling the interview can sometimes be difficult and requires skill. For example: a person may be high on the Predictors of Selling Skills and Persuasive Power (SS&PP) and Communications-Oral (CO). These people can sneak control of the interview away from you. Just because they do that, you may not want to think of them as a negative. They may be strong people for jobs in, for example, sales or customer relations.

Catching the Con Artist

One other example of a candidate that can sneak control away from you and win the job is the major league con artist and liar. These con people usually have excellent appearances, are smooth talkers, and have no trouble winning jobs. Con artist types have proven they can fool very sharp people. The good news is that if you follow my selection system (from resume screen to reference check), you will likely catch the con artist before you make a costly hiring mistake. When you catch the con, you and the interviewing team will experience jubilation and enjoy a smile.

The Master Interviewer's Eight Principles of Interview Control

First Principle—Preparation

The first principle in keeping control is preparation. Have all documentation gathered and in front of you when the candidate comes in:

Resume

TeleScreen

Any notes

Prewritten Predictor Interview Guide with candidate's name at the top

File folder with candidate's name on it

When the candidates see how organized you are, they will feel you are a pro who knows what you are doing. Good applicants will appreciate this; con artists will start getting the worried look.

Controlling the Wanders and Talkers

The first rule in controlling wanderers and talkers is to tell them to please relate their answers to specifics of past job experiences. Do not let them answer in generalities or by telling you how to do it; stop them immediately and say, "tell me specifically what you actually did." Then ask, "What were the results?" Frequently it is necessary to tell them, **"I am not interested in how to do it, only in the specifics of what you did"**.

The Pen is Mightier than the Ink

When the candidate rambles, you can just *lay your pen down*. They will see that what they are saying is so unimportant you have stopped taking notes. When they start giving you relevant information, then you pick up your pen again. A strong body language signal for the rambling or the flowery conversationalist is for you to leave the room while they are rambling.—(Sorry, I was just rambling and having fun getting you to think about ways to gain control.)

Second Principle—Shut-up to Learn

The number one reason candidates do not give adequate information is that the interviewer talks too much. Oh sure, you never do that. We all do it; feel better?

The number one reason interviewers talk too much is because they do not have their Predictor Interview Guide written out. Without written questions, the interviewer just starts telling the candidate about the glories of the job, the company, themselves, and rambling war stories.

How Much Should You Talk?

The number two reason that candidates do not talk enough is because the interviewee does not want to interrupt the interviewer who is happy doing all the talking. If you are like me and love to talk, then remember four words that will help you solve your problem and get the interviewee to talk. The four power words are: **Shut Up and Listen**. You should shut up during 75% of the interview. More politely phrased, you should be listening during 75% of the interview.

> *Paullin's Point—Nothing encourages the candidate to talk more than silence. You cannot learn decision making information about the applicant while you are talking.*

Another way to get the candidate to talk more is to use follow-up questions such as:

Can you tell me more about…?

What exactly were the results of…?

How did your manager feel about…?

Please go into the specifics of…

> *Paullin's Point—If you just leave a little silence, the candidate will feel the need to start filling in the silence by sharing more information.*

Third Principle—Fishing; Catch and Release: Interviewing; Pry and Release!

If you have to pry information from the candidate then you may want to "pry and release." The candidate has not volunteered the information I need to know and this causes me to wish to say, **"Thank you very little, and you are free to go."**

Fourth Principle—Yes and NO Questioning

Ivory tower minds will tell you that you should not ask close-ended questions because the candidate can simply answer with a yes or no. If the candidate does that very often, this will simply tell you that they do not have the good judgment or communication skills to give you more information. The candidate who only gives yes or no answers is indicating how they will answer customers or company personnel after being hired. It is best to ask open-ended questions, but sprinkling in a few closed questions will add to the seasoning. If you need more data than the applicant gives, then simply use follow-ups such as, "Please tell me more about…."

Fifth Principle—Listen for "Feathers"

The key is to listen for data. Are they giving you hard specific data on how they performed that job with results or are they giving you "feathers?" The way to test for "feathers" is to listen to their lack of specifics, lack of enthusiasm, lack of emotions, and what they don't say.

After you ask a question, shut up, and let the candidate answer. So many interviewers ask the question, then restate it, and then clarify it. Just ask the question and listen. In listening to answers, you will learn to judge what a good answer is and what a mediocre answer is. You will also learn to judge when a candidate has no positive data to give you on the question because they are giving you some type of ambiguous reply or silence. If you do not get the data sought in the question, then the candidate is probably weak in that area. Silence is deafening. Let the silence happen, and the candidate will talk and provide you with data.

> ***Paullin's Point—If the candidate does not break the silence, that silence should break your eardrums with data.***

Sixth Principle—Shocking News!

If the applicant starts revealing information that seems shocking, horrible, or even funny, control yourself and listen. The applicant may reveal more important information to help you in your decision.

Seventh Principle—Ending the Interview

A major part of controlling the interview is knowing exactly how you are going to end it. To avoid this awkward moment write down the words that you are going to say for ending the interview and use them. *"It has been nice talking to you, Ms. Jones. I will be looking at several other candidates before I make my decision on who I will hire (or interview again). If you do not hear from me by _____, then you probably will not. Thanks for coming in, and I wish you good luck."* Stand up and walk them to the door— it's over.

Eighth Principle—Extending the Interview

The exception to ending the interview this way is when you have a superior candidate, and you wish to extend the interview time to learn more information.

Express your interest to the candidate with questions such as, "Are you available to talk to us further?" or, "If we make you an offer, when will you be able to start?" After asking these questions, act! Invite the candidate back for more interviews, check his references, and if all works out, make him the job offer.

Summary

It is necessary to control the interview if you want to pick the best candidate. The first rule in controlling the interview is to control yourself. Be ready and prepared with all materials when the candidate arrives. Follow your Predictor Interview Guide, but do not lose the spontaneity of being able to bring in additional questions and use follow-up questions. Do not "over-talk" the applicant. SHUT UP AND LISTEN at least 75% of the time. Know ways to get the applicant to talk more, to talk in specifics, and get specific results. You do not want to hear about job descriptions, generalities, or this is how you do that. You need the specifics of what the candidate actually did.

Spend the time to write down and practice your close. This will replace that awkward moment with a comfortable close. Being prepared and in control from beginning to end will show the candidate that you are a professional manager.

Candidates may even compliment you on your interview unless they are the con artist who will have had a hard time painting a false picture for you. This is no con: be prepared, listen and you will have control. "Shut up" and the silence created will be filled by the candidate telling you decision making data.

> *Practice does not make perfect; perfect practice makes perfect.—*
> *Vince Lombardi*

22

Interpreting Answers— What Does That Mean?

The Interpretation of Answers Allows Hiring the Best

You have defined the Predictors that fit your job description, and have written questions for your Predictor Interview Guide. You are now ready to ask them of the applicant.

During the interview, as the applicant answers your questions, record the answer in your own shorthand. Writing the answers during the interview prevents forgetting what the applicant said as well as confusing one candidate's answers with another's. **(Do it faithfully because very few of us ever have total recall. I forgot the title of the memory course I took!)** Now that you have the candidate's answers, you must be able to interpret them, and give a quantitative score. When you can score an answer of a Predictor, you will be able to give the candidate a score on the total questions for that Predictor.

Everything seems to have quantitative measurements: Baseball = runs, basketball = points, cars = miles per hour, and golf = strokes. For interviewing we will use numbers and words. Understand the quantitative scoreboard for interviewing, because it will help you to compare the applicants and select the best when several are good.

Predictor Score Cards

The Predictor Score Card is a rating scale on answers, other data and the applicant's total and final rating.

Predictor Rating Scale		
Rating	**Word Rating**	**Explanation**
5 or A	Exceptional	Walks on water
4 or B	Superior	Walks on water, but gets ankles wet
3 or C	Average	Swims in water
2 or D	Below Average	Sinks in water
1 or F	Not Hirable or Acceptable	Already drowned
0	The interviewer or the judge wasn't at the pool (received no good or bad data on the candidate- It neither helps nor hurts the candidate)	

The Rule of 3

It is imperative to understand that the numeric scores are based on a value of 3 as being an average successful employee. **I have found it helpful to relate the Rule of 3 to an actual successful employee in your organization.** You should be able to name this person and all interviewers should agree on who this person is. So if your candidate gives 3 answers and the overall rating is a 3, the applicant is a good hire and this indicates he or she will be an average, successful employee. If the applicant's total ranking is a 4 or 5, then you will have a person who will most likely be a high achiever. If you hire a 2 or a 1, then you will probably end up firing him, or by keeping him, have an inferior producing employee.

Your job as a manager is to hire the best people; hopefully people even better than yourself. If you do this and your company is smart, they will see you putting together highly productive teams, and you will get promoted because of your team and management skills. A manager who hires superior people that are "superstars" should be promoted. A manager who continuously hires average people that can be controlled easily should certainly not be promoted.

After you have interviewed the applicant, then grade each Predictor you've used. Remember, some Predictors will be more critical than others. Any information that you have gathered (e.g., reference checks) can also be used to numerically score a Predictor. Look at the big picture of your scores for the candidate and come up with an overall score.

The 5 Treasure Chests of Hiring Data
1. **Assessment of the resume**
2. **TeleScreens**
3. **Candidate observations during interview**
4. **Reference Checks**
5. **Candidate's follow-up skills**

Your Predictor Score Card

Your Predictor Score Cards are especially helpful when you end up with two candidates you like equally. You cannot hire both and must make a decision because there is only one position. By looking at the Predictors, it will usually show one candidate to be slightly stronger in the critical Predictors than the others.

The Predictor Score Card should also be saved for EEO documentation. Your documentation will show you measured the candidates with a system; explain why the candidate was not hired; and show how you based your selection. This demonstrates you had a fair system for all applicants and based your decision on job-related data, not unrelated data such as race, creed, gender, etc.

Now you have an overall score on the applicant. If you are considering hiring the person, then it must be assumed that they are ranked as a 3, 4, or 5. It is best to have two other managers interview the applicant so that you can get their feedback and scores. The other managers should meet with you to discuss the candidate for the purpose of ranking the candidate by Predictors and for an overall Predictor Score Card grade.

PREDICTOR SCORECARD

Candidate:_____   Position:_____

Evaluation Code

5 Exceptional
4 Superior
3 Average
2 Below Average
1 Not Hirable
0 Insufficient Data

RATER: **RATING**	**Tom**	**Dick**	**Mary**	**Total**
AP: Attendance Punctuality	5	4	5	4.7
AUL: Ability to understand and learn	4	5	5	4.7
CO: Communication Oral	5	5	5	5
CS: Computer Skills	4	4	3	3.7
CW: Communication Written	4	5	4	4.3
IPS: Interpersonal Skills	4	4	4	4
POT: Planning, Organization & Time Mgmt	5	5	5	5
RSP: Responsiveness	5	4	5	4.7
SM: Self Motivation	4	4	4	4
WE: Work Ethics	4	4	5	4.3
TOTAL	4.4	4.4	4.5	4.4

Summary

You have learned a grading scale to evaluate the applicant's answers quantitatively. The scale is based on the candidate's answers compared to your average successful person on that job who you have identified as a 3. An applicant with an overall rating of 3 should produce an average successful person on the job. A candidate with a rating of 4 or 5 should produce superior results. A candidate will have different scores on different Predictors, and an overall rating will be determined.

You now have their batting average, yards per carry or points per game and you make the decision of putting them on your team. Finally, the documentation by Predictors also provides you with documentation of a fair system should a discrimination suit arise.

After your scoring and the Team Evaluation Process, you can now hire the best and reap the rewards of higher productivity, high morale, higher raises, and possibly be promoted.

Your Hiring Firing Experts Notes:

23

Follow-up Questions that Reveal

Detective Colombo Questioning Predicts the Best Hire

Colombo the detective questioned people in a relaxed manner that would prove some people innocent and always find the guilty party. The questions were provocative about behavior toward the job description which was the crime. It was his empathic listening to the answers that solved every mystery. Equally important was his ability to use follow-up questions to obtain more information on the subject.

Follow-up Like Detective Columbo

Follow-up questions are not used after every interviewing question, only when more information would be helpful. Have follow-ups in your head at the ready. For example:

Can you tell me more about…?

How did you do?

How did you feel about that?

Would you give more details on…?

Give me a specific example at XYZ when you accomplished this.

Please be more specific and describe what occurred.

Interesting, tell me more.

What did your boss say?

What were the outcomes?

Describe what happened then.

Please explain more.

How did your company react?

Did you receive any accolades for this?

Can you give me more examples?

Follow-up questions tend to draw the candidate out, many times catching the liar or the smooth-talker who is just giving you feathers of data. It is my experience good candidates do well with follow-up questions, but poor applicants become uncomfortable and have difficulty in giving specifics and details.

Follow-up questions are easy to use. By commanding a few spontaneous follow-ups, you can greatly enhance your interviewing power to get helpful data on making better decisions.

24

Reference Checking—The Validator or Terminator?

Paullin's Point—A bad reference check is as hard to find as a good employee.

Reference Check$ Mean Real Dollar$

A manager who does not have time to do reference checks may soon not have to worry about time spent on being a manager. To put this more bluntly, if you do not do reference checks, you are putting your career and company at great risk! Most likely, reference checks will confirm the positive data you gathered during interviews and allow you to sleep well after hiring the person. Reference and background checks can save you from hiring the thief, rapist, murderer, doper, drinker, or the bad employee. Those examples are dramatic but real. Less dramatic may be to discover the person has bad attendance or is not able to get along with people. At this point, we should be in agreement: reference checks are mandatory for every position from the loading dock to the executive suite.

Who does the Reference Checks?

Reference checking is the responsibility of the hiring manager, and if you are the hiring manager, you should do it. If you have to, delegate it to someone who knows what to look for and is trained to do it. However, this is a key position. I recommend the hiring manager do it because the hiring manager will live with the hiring decision and the person's future performance.

Secrets Must be Kept

You must state up front to the reference that this is a confidential reference check and its content will not be discussed with the applicant. As the hiring manager, if you have the appropriate title of importance to match the person at the other end, it makes it more likely to gain cooperation.

> *Paullin's Point—Networking Via Reference Checks: I have known executives that have called other executives for a reference check, and it has ended up in a further conversation of how their businesses could work with each other. I have also seen where the reference becomes a hire. Call this networking via reference checks.*

I recommend reference checks be done as soon as you have finished the final interview. **Yes, as soon as you have finished the final interview.** You may do this before the other interviewing managers interview. The two main reasons to do reference checking as soon as you have finished the final interview are: Negative data may turn up that **KO's** the candidate. For example, the candidate had substandard sales and was pressured into resigning. If this is a knockout, you've saved the time of the other two managers. Positive data confirms the decision to have other managers interview.

There are arguments for doing reference checks after all the interviews are complete and even after you extend the offer. Despite these arguments, decide when and who should do the reference checks, but *never* decide if they should be done. They **must be done** and it absolutely should be company policy.

Background Checks

Today there are services, which provide background checks ranging from credit to criminal checks and things in between such as job and salary history. As long as it is a legal investigation and is job related, then it is a consideration.

Reference checks may save you from a felon, but more likely, reference checks will alert you to problems such as the person who cannot get along with customers or fellow employees. Reference checks usually will confirm the positive data you have from your interview.

Human Resources—No! No! No!

Human resource departments do not give the references a hiring manager needs. This is their policy for liability reasons. The larger the company, the more likely this will be found true. However, most human resource departments will verify some of the following:

Verify or confirm employment and dates employed

Verify position or positions held

Verify final salary

That is usually all you will get from H.R. departments.

It is unlikely that you will get a human resource manager that will give you a lot of information. Do not get discouraged and go first to your best source—the immediate manager who actually knows your candidate personally and his work performance.

Go to Their Boss

I use the candidate's references only when they are their former managers. I want to talk to the people that have managed the candidate. I do not want their friend, teacher, coach, or pastor. Candidates may tend to give what I call their mother and father references...these references are guaranteed to give you positive data.

Your mission is to talk to the person's former managers. You can make this happen during the interview. As you go through the interview, at each place of employment, ask the candidate whom he reported to... get the name, and then ask would he use them as a reference? If he gives you the name of the person, then and only then, ask him for the phone number or to get you the phone number. **If he would not use the person as a reference, you must use the follow-up question...tell me why?**

Breaking the HR No Reference Roadblock

The candidate's immediate manager may also have been schooled by the human resources department to not give references. I have usually found that I still can get these people to talk if I plan carefully what I am going to say.

> **I say something like this to the manager:**
>
> *"As a manager I understand that your only legal concerns are with a bad reference. However, if a person has done a good job for me I feel I owe them a good reference. I have no risk in giving a 'good' reference; therefore, I am happy to give them for good employees. So, I am assuming that if you are unable to give me a reference it is because the reference would be very negative. Could you help me by answering a few questions about _____ _____ (applicant's name)?"*

Usually after this, the manager tells me that the candidate is good and that it is just policy, and once that curtain has been opened, he will go on to tell me more things.

If I do the same thing and the manager who has negative data and had a bad experience with the candidate responds with a "no comment" or "I have nothing to say to you," I may try other questions. If I keep getting the "no comments" I then say that I get the picture. I may ask, "Did the candidate leave on his own?" If I then get a "No comment," I think I have some data that gives me a red flag.

> *Paullin's Point—I can almost tell by the curtness and tone if a manager is negative about a former employee. Conversely, good references are usually friendly in tone and the manager wants to do the former employee a favor.*

The Watch Out Reference—Current Employer

In the interview, always ask the candidate if they would use their current manager for a reference. Normally they will say no, and then you must find out why. It is usually because the current company does not know they are looking. If that is the case, you have an option. You ask the employee, "If we reach an agreement, would you be willing to be hired contingent on your reference check with your current company bearing out what you are telling us?" Then ask him what his manager will tell us when queried?

A good candidate may have had a jerk manager and that must be taken into consideration. But, if a candidate has had three jobs and nobody will give me a reference, then some red flags go up.

Guidelines for doing a Successful Reference Check

> **Go to Chapter 30 for TeleReference guidelines, instructions and example.**

Summary

Reference checks validate each preceding step in the interview process. Reference checks may also eliminate the candidate. If you want to be the manager who produces the highest turnover, then do not take the time to do those valuable reference checks. In fact, a manager who has the responsibility but does not do the reference checks, and ends up with a bad hire should be reprimanded. This sounds extreme, but it demonstrates the importance I feel about reference checks. Get your reference checks accomplished; avoid potential problems; and sleep well.

Your Hiring Firing Experts Notes:

25

Team Interviewing For Best Hires

The Team Evaluation Process

Ideally, three managers should be in the interviewing process: The hiring manager, the hiring manager's boss, and another manager who is familiar with the position being filled. All interviewing managers should also understand the interviewing process and be able to share their data gained during their interview in a structured team data sharing process. Three managers are ideal because three heads are better than one, and any more than three provides an unmanageable crowd for data sharing.

Do not over cook the candidate with interviews. All key players of the company may meet the candidate, but not everyone needs to interview the person.

Each manager assigned to interview the candidate should be given the Predictor Interview Guide and Predictors that he or she is to use for questioning the applicant during the interview. Each Predictor should ideally have at least two managers gathering data. Important Predictors and more difficult Predictors to assess, such as Judgment (J), should be assigned to all interviewing managers. A Predictor such as Ability to Understand and Learn (AUL), that may be easier to evaluate, can be handled by one or two managers.

Data Sharing

It is a good idea to have the hiring manager's boss as a part of the data sharing team if it is understood that he is not to wear the "boss hat" during the data sharing meeting. All data sharing managers must be equal for data sharing or else it will turn into a power struggle, and the one with the most rank, rather than the strong hiring data will prevail.

Check Guns and Egos at the Door

Differing views must be encouraged to bring out all data. The dissenting view must be acknowledged, and the manager thanked and **never** put down or discouraged. Using the Predictor rating scale as described in **Chapter 22**, a chart can be made that will have the candidate's name on it, and the Predictors written down vertically, preferably in order of importance. The reason that I say preferably in order of importance is simply that it is difficult to decide on exact importance. It is possible to label about the first 2 to 5 Predictors as being more critical to job success. Horizontally, the names of the interviewers go across the top.

> *Paullin's Point—Managers should never discuss the candidate until their Predictor scores have been written down and the data sharing session has begun.*

It is important that the managers not be influenced by each other until they have written down their scores and are ready to discuss the Predictors. After each manager has written down his scores for the individual Predictors, then a discussion is held for each Predictor. After discussing the Predictors, a final score is reached for that candidate on that specific Predictor. This process is repeated for each Predictor.

At the end of evaluating each specific Predictor then each interviewer gives a short summation of the candidate and a final numeric score, which represents his overall hiring evaluation of the candidate. This summation becomes part of the documentation.

After all managers have given and discussed their overall ratings, a final numeric rating should be given to the candidate. Normally the hiring manager then takes the scores on the final candidates, discusses them with the group, and makes a decision on which candidate will be given the offer.

From legal and record keeping standpoints, it is important that all data sheets on all candidates be saved. If a discrimination charge is filed, then you have records to verify that all candidates had an equal opportunity and were judged under the same system. From a promotion standpoint, the interview guides and the data gained can become very important resources in developing and considering the candidate for other positions in the future.

Summary

The Team Evaluation Process helps give the hiring manager the insights of others in order to get a better hire than if done alone. It is best done by three managers who understand the position and the system. The hiring manager's boss should be included in the interviewing and the data sharing process. The data sharing must not become an ego or power struggle. Egos and guns should be checked at the door, because the data sharing process must not become a struggle of who is right and wrong. Differing opinions should be encouraged and the managers thanked but never put down.

After the Predictors are rated, a final decision is made regarding each candidate's overall hireability. The hiring manager then takes the data on all candidates, discusses with the group and makes a decision on which candidate will be given the offer.

> *Paullin's Point—The same numeric evaluation system can be used for hiring, performance appraisals, and for firing.*

All records should be maintained for possible litigation and for future promotions.

Your Hiring Firing Experts Notes:

26

Rejection Letters that Don't Humiliate

A.S.S. Letters

Mine are called Appreciation but Still Searching Letters or A.S.S. letters. These can be sent out at different stages in the selection process or at the end, it is up to you.

Here is an example:

Dear:

We've appreciated meeting you and having the opportunity to interview you. We've decided to continue to interview candidates who we feel more closely meet our needs for this position. We will keep your credentials on file for consideration of other openings. In the meantime we wish you success in your job search.

Sincerely,

In your selection system, there should be points in the process where you do send out letters of status (the bulk of these letters are turndown letters).

Turndown letters should be tactfully done, where they do not actually reject the person, but rather let them know that you have appreciated them and that you have decided that you will continue the search for the position. You will also keep them in mind and wish them success in their career search.

I do believe that all candidates that are interviewed in person do deserve a letter of status and that large corporations that have resources should send letters of status to everyone. The small business person or sales manager that does not have help in answering the 300 resumes e-mailed in should not be burdened with guilt if every resume does not receive a written response. I have known companies and managers who have spent countless hours making sure every applicant who sent in a resume received some sort of reply. Is that the best use of your time?

I personally stopped replying to every candidate years ago, and have saved countless hours, which I in turn have invested in the people that I have hired. Incidentally, I have received few complaints or inquiries from not responding to all applicants. If you and your staff have time, respond to all, and sleep well. If not, selectively respond, and live with a little guilt and some extra hours of saved time. I am not insensitive; I just do not have enough time to do everything, but yet, I have all the time there is in 24 hours. Once I learned that I cannot do everything that I am supposed to do, I set my priorities, and now only do the things that pay the biggest dividends. I send letters or e-mails on a selective basis.

Love Your Human Resources Department

You are now getting the feeling that I do not spend a lot of my time on the human resource practice and commonly held opinion that every applicant needs a letter of status. This human resource opinion is theoretically right, and I've known HR people who feel strongly about this. HR people can be of great assistance to managers, which includes writing and sending letters of offer or turndown. HR people can be your greatest advisors and best supporters when hiring and firing.

Paullin's Point—A manager who has an HR department as a resource and does not use it, is in the same TUNNEL OF INFLEXIBILTY as the manager who does not see how technical innovations can improve a business. Indeed, there is a light at the end of this TUNNEL...but, it is a train.

More of the Story

I must say I discovered how helpful the HR department could be while working with a Fortune 200 company. As a sales manager, I was virtually responsible for the total selection process, but company guidelines were supposed to be followed. One of the policies was that all resumes were to receive a letter of status, but I had no secretary or word processor to complete this Herculean task.

One time I was just too busy and never got around to sending around 300 letters of status to applicants. Guess what happened? Virtually nothing except that I saved about four hours of my life. I invested that time in more important things, from sales training of my new hire to sailing with my son, Devin. Whether the investment of the four hours was for business or pleasure, it was worth more than the four hours invested in status and turndown letters.

The next time I hired, I took the gamble again. I did not spend the four hours usually required to send out the letters and once again, nothing happened. I also had learned that if I did send out the 300 letters, some applicants would call and ask me why I did not interview or hire them. These calls were time consuming, defensive, and could have resulted in legal issues. So, if I did not send the letters, I saved time and energy.

The Human Resource Department From Heaven or Hell?

I decided to test this particular company policy and continued not to send any applicants letters of rejection. It was a year before I went public with my time-saving secret. It happened that one of my peers was complaining about the time spent on sending rejection letters, and all other managers cried with him, except smiling me. I shared my secret with them and most of the managers followed my lead, with the exception of one manager who decided to check it out and shared my secret with human resources.

Subsequently, I was called on the human resource carpet and it was explained to me how not sending letters was an infringement on the company's HR policy and public relations. With great sweat and a knot in my stomach, I announced that I was sorry, but that I just did not have the time to do this task.

I was prepared to do verbal warfare with who I thought would be the HR "man from hell" and imagined the negative affect this would have on my personnel file. An amazing thing happened, however. I learned how valuable a resource an HR department could be. The HR man was heaven sent and said that he understood the time constraints of field managers and his department would be happy to send letters for me. All I had to do was send the HR department the rejected resumes.

HR Department Heaven

I asked the "HR man (now) from heaven" if there were any other ways that human resources could help me. The human resource revelation and revival was born, and this sinner was saved. The HR department was available to help me, and I used everything. HR was available to: write and place ads, screen resumes, aid in interviewing, write and send rejection letters…on and on. In order to get this help, I had to do one thing—call HR and request it. What an economical price to pay! I used this valuable resource and, needless to say, they became one of my favorite departments.

If available to you, use your HR department, they are professionals and can help you in countless ways.

27

The Job Offer—Party Now!

The Fruit of Your Efforts

After going through the selection process and making a decision to hire a candidate, you have made quite an investment in time and resources. Everything you have done to this point has been designed to land the best candidate and now culminates in making the successful offer and a joyous celebration.

You must create an environment consistent with the environment you created throughout the interview process—but now the candidate is on the team. Now you want to give the candidate that important message that you have made your decision and he or she is your choice. The message should be clear that, **"We want you in our organization; we believe you can help us achieve our goals; and your future is best served by choosing to be with us."**

Role Reversal

The candidate has been selling since the first stage of the interviewing process, and now there is a gradual shift toward the hiring company to close the sale by selling the candidate on joining and having a career with the company.

During the interview, information and data should have been gained about the salary that is fair to the applicant and the company. This is easily done by asking the candidate what their current salary is, and asking what they made at other positions. The salary history, plus your own judgment of your position and its market value should give you an indication of the money needed that is fair and that will land the candidate.

You may wish to take the candidate to dinner, and he or she may bring his or her significant other. A dinner or lunch with both parties provides an opportunity to meet the significant other and gives you further insight on what it takes to make the candidate happy. You can accomplish a lot by selling the company and learn a lot during this dinner. A negative significant other can ruin the deal, and a positive one can help make the deal and reduce the possibility of turnover.

The degree of the message will vary. The principal of the message is similar whether it is an administrative assistant or CEO. You let the candidate know his or her importance and that he or she is valued. It is important that before the final offer is extended, you have settled on all employment terms and have a good idea that the candidate will accept the offer.

The "ballpark" salary and benefits have usually been discussed with the candidate, and an informal agreement has been reached before the formal offer is made. In many positions, the offer can be made over the phone, but in some positions, because of the importance of the position and any possibility of further negotiations, the offer will be best served by meeting in person and made in writing

Presuming that during the interview process an informal agreement is reached on terms, then I ask the candidate and significant other out for dinner.

I meet with the candidate privately before dinner and present the written offer. Included in this letter is the message of congratulations and welcome aboard. Then the dinner is used as a celebration dinner, and the purpose is to show the new hire and significant other the important role and the great career available in the organization. If a dinner is not possible or appropriate, a lunch can be used for the same purpose.

After the offer has been accepted, another way to recognize your new hire is with an e-mail blast. An e-mail of congratulations and welcome aboard can be sent to team members before or in the first few days of employment. In turn, you should encourage your key players to send your new hire e-mails of congratulations and welcome aboard.

Summary

The celebration dinner or lunch resells the candidate and significant other on how happy you and the company are that he or she is coming on board and that a great career decision has been made. Reselling the candidate can make a lasting impression. This helps commit the candidate to your company and lessens the chances of future turnover.

All your efforts culminate in the employment offer and a celebration for all. How the offer is made can make the difference in which company the candidate selects and lessens the prospect of turnover once hired.

Your Hiring Firing Experts Notes:

28

Bringing the New Hire On Board

The First Days and Weeks are Critical

The time and effort put into acquainting your new employee the first days and weeks on the job are critical to their retention and success. This includes acquainting the new employee with the overall company, his or her staff, specifics of the office, and mentor.

Before the New Hire Arrives

Develop a pre-arrival checklist, for example, involving work space, telephone, PC, mail, and supplies. Other steps to take before the new hire's first day may be to order business cards, nameplate, company credit card, and cell phone. A written announcement to the staff of the new hire's arrival and responsibilities may also be distributed

Day One

Greet the new hire the first day, and if required, arrange a meeting with HR and introduce associates. Tour the department and building, and take the new hire to lunch that first day. Review department policy and procedures and company policy and procedures if this has not been done by HR. Most importantly, we encourage the review of the job description, job objectives, and expectations.

Job Responsibilities and Performance

The new employee's job description should be thoroughly reviewed and discussed to answer questions and ensure understanding. Measurable goals and targeted objectives need to be established that will be reviewed and measured on a quarterly and annual basis.

The performance management and appraisal system should be introduced, and the employee should receive training both as a person who will be evaluated and as a manager who writes evaluations in the event the new employee is supervising people. Also, the salary administration program should be reviewed, including the sales compensation plan for those in sales.

Meeting Key Players

You may also want to set-up meetings with key executives and players with whom the new employee supports and/or interacts. You may serve as the one who makes the introduction and you may want to precede this with a copy of the new employee's resume. This can be done over several weeks so that it accommodates everyone's schedules.

Summary

By having an On-Boarding plan and taking these steps, you help ensure a faster start on the job. This has been shown to increase loyalty and reduce turnover.

PART V

Paullin's Hiring Firing Experts Tool Kit

29

Your Performance Predictors and Example Questions

Here are Performance Predictors and listed under each Predictor are example questions. Customize these in your Predictor Interview Guide for your specific job description and the candidate's actual work experience and background.

Core Performance Predictors are listed first. It has been my experience that these Core Performance Predictors should be the basis for most interview questions that candidates in management are asked.

Following this list are other Performance Predictors and questions that you may want to include in the interview.

Paullin's Point—Remember your questions should tap the candidate's specific work experience and background. You want the candidate to tell you "what they've done," not tell you "how to do it."

Key instruction: Customize each question to the candidate's specific work experience. For example in the questions below, substitute the specific company name or position you are asking the candidate about in place of "...." or ABC, XYZ, etc.

Core Performance Predictors and Questions
AUL: Ability to Understand & Learn

What were the most challenging things you had to learn on your jobs at ABC and DEF? Tell me about how you managed to accomplish these? What were the results?

How did you learn your job at ABC?

How did you learn your product knowledge at ABC?

How did you learn the technical portion of your job at ABC?

What was the hardest thing you had to learn at ABC?

How did you learn it?

How did you learn to use the software at ABC?

What courses in ……..did you do your best in? Which courses did you have the most difficulty in?

What will your college transcript show your grade point average to be? Can you send us a copy of your transcript? (This "puts the ball in their court" to take personal responsibility for making sure the transcript is sent.)

CO: Communication Skills Oral

The best data on Communication Skills Oral come from how the candidate communicates during the TeleScreen and during the actual interview. Do they speak clearly and make their points? Listen for utterances, words and phrases such as "Ah," "Um," "Like," "You Know" and needless hesitations between and in mid-sentence.

What opportunities have you had to speak before groups of people?

What were your grades in speech and communication classes?

Tell me about seminars or group discussions you've led.

Give me examples of when you have had to demonstrate platform skills.
Were you ever on stage? What was your role?

Did you take debate in high school or college? How did you do?

What is the largest group that you have ever spoken to? How did you feel? How did you do?

What business presentations have you made? What feedback did you receive?

What public speaking have you done?

How do you communicate orally with your team?

Give me an example of how you verbally responded to negative criticism from a boss?

CS:Computer Skills
Computer skills are essential to the candidate's success in today's business.

What software do you use to manage and keep things going on your job?

What software are you proficient in?

How did you learn the software at your company? How would you assess its effectiveness?

Tell me how you made your most important spreadsheets at ABC.

What data base programs do you use to organize and report results?

CW: Communication Skills Written
Tell me about the RFPs that you have written?

What written business plans (reports, etc.) have you done for ABC and for EFG?

What grade did you receive in English? Creative writing?

What business proposals have you been in charge of?

What has been your most challenging written document?

What else have you written that would give me an indication of your writing skills?

Were you responsible for any written materials at ABC?

What did your manager say about your written reports and written communication skills?

INT: Integrity
Typically you will not ask direct questions on integrity and telling the truth. As a skilled interviewer, however, you will almost always catch people with low integrity stumbling and making mistakes during the regular interview process. A skilled interviewer will use follow-up questions to gain more information and may also catch people with low integrity.

Another way to gain integrity data is after asking questions about degrees, grades or performance appraisals, follow-up by asking the candidate if he will email or send copies. If the candidate doesn't, it may indicate he lied about the information or just does not follow-up on commitments. In any case, it is a red flag.

Would you send me a copy of your transcript, performance appraisal, CPA certificate, etc.?

Tell me about a time when you have had to explain your business dealings?

When have your expenses ever been questioned?

Have you ever had to explain any unethical business happenings?

We all have to go around policy to get by. When have you gone outside the rules?

You said Mr. Jones was your manager at ABC and that we could use him as a reference. When we call him, why will he say you left? What will he tell us about your ending salary? About your attendance? About your sales ranking?

IPS: Interpersonal Skills

Look for positive or negative descriptions to see how the candidate gets along with people. High interpersonal skill people will talk during the interview about how they like people.

What do you enjoy most about your work? Your business?

Will the people you worked with at ABC describe you as an introvert or extrovert? Why do you think you are described this way?

Have you ever been elected or selected to any business positions that you would like to tell me about?

When we ask your manager at ABC to tell us how you got along with people, what will he or she say?

Tell me about the people at ABC that you worked closely with. How about the people you worked with at DEF?

Contrast your managers at ABC and DEF?

What leadership positions have you held in business? How did you get them?

Give me the names of the two people that you work most closely with and tell me about them?

Why are you applying for this job?
If it is a people oriented job, listen to see how the candidate talks about people (love people, like talking to people).

Tell me about a time when you have gone out of your way for others in your company?

What are some of your key customers like at ABC?

JDG: Judgment

Tell me about your biggest business risks and how they worked out?

Have you ever had a time when you had to make that "big decision" without help? Tell me about it.

What were your toughest business decisions at ABC and DEF?

Have you ever gone against the company direction?

What are the most profitable business decisions that you have made?

When were you on the spot about an issue? What did you do? What were the results?

MS&L: Management Skills & Leadership

Management Skills & Leadership and Interpersonal Skills are related and may have similar questions.

How did you get your team to do what was needed?

Tell me about some challenging projects and how you managed through them? How did you get your team to buy in?

How do your employees know how they are doing?

Have you ever been elected to any positions that you would like to tell me about? (Also applies to interpersonal skills)

Tell me about a time when you implemented a strategic plan with your people?

What positions of leadership have you held at ABC? At DEF?

Have you held any other positions where you have directed others that you would like to tell me about? Tell me about some of the results that stand out in your mind?

Were you promoted at ABC? Did this entail managing others?

What did you do to make sure the new job was a successful move? What were the results?

What positions have you held where you managed others? How did you do?

How did you implement your plans at ABC? How did you get others to go along?

Describe how you planned your last staff meeting.

How do you manage to "get it all done?" (Did the candidate use their team and delegate?)

How do you get your employees to do more?

When you need to plan a major program, what steps do you take? (See how candidates involve their people.)

When you had a problem employee, what did you do? Can you give me a specific example?

Give me some examples of your leadership results?

What are your best managerial skills? Why?

What have you defined as your most critical tools for managerial success?

What were your biggest managerial challenges? How did you go about accomplishing these? What were the results?

How did you set plans for your teams at ABC?

How do you go about making budget?

Have you ever had to cut expenses, cut budget or downsize? Tell me about it.

What are the biggest challenges you faced as a manager? What did you do?

Tell me about your biggest managerial accomplishments?

How do you set your own goals? How did you go about making them happen? Examples?

How do *you know* how your employees are doing? How do *they know* how they are doing?

How do you evaluate your managers and people?

How have you judged progress on some of your management projects?

How do you measure performance of your employees?

How do you incent/reward average employees? Below standard employees? Above standard employees?

POT: Planning, Organizing & Time Management

Listen for planning ahead, written plans, making lists, working from To-Do lists, scheduling, and working by priorities. An important example of this is what the candidate brings to the interview; extra resumes, references, transcripts, special reports, awards, certificates, etc.

Tell me about some key deadlines that you had the responsibility for at ABC?

How many times did you miss deadlines?

What did you do to prepare for this interview?

Did you look our company up on the web? What did you learn? What did you like?

How do you start your work day at ABC? How do you start your week at ABC?

Is there anything that you brought to this interview that you would like to show me?

You have a lot going on at ABC, how do you juggle all the balls without letting them fall to the floor?

You have a lot of responsibilities at ABC. How do you keep things going?

How did you decide on what you were going to work on this week at ABC?

How do you go about starting to work on a project?

What responsibilities do you currently have at ABC that involve project planning? Tell me a specific example.

Tell me about the most critical plan that you have been in charge of at ABC?

How did you control things under your direction at ABC?

What are the techniques you use in managing your time?

What tools do you use to keep yourself organized at ABC? How does that work?

Describe a typical day at ABC.

How did you set your priorities at ABC?

PS: Platform Skills
Platform Skills and Communication Skills Oral are related and may have similar questions.

What speeches have you given that you are proud of?

What seminars have you led? What were the results?

Tell me about some workshops that you have led?

Have you ever been rated by your audience or group? What were the results?

Tell me about any speeches that you have given?

What is the longest speech that you have given? What was the objective? What were the results?

What audio and visual aids do you use when speaking and how do you use them?

Tell me about how you've used Power Point in your presentations? Did you do this all by yourself or did you receive help?

How have you handled a difficult person in the audience?

R&D: Risk Taking and Decisiveness
Risk Taking & Decisiveness and Judgment are related and may have similar questions.

What is the biggest business decision that you made at ABC? At DEF?

What gamble did you take at ABC? Did it pay?

What is the most important decision that you have made in the past five years? What were the results?

Have you ever made a business decision that was not yours to make? How were the fences mended after doing this?

Have you ever disagreed with your manager? How did you approach him or her? What were the results?

Tell me about the biggest business risks that you have taken.

What new ideas have you presented to your past companies? What were the results?

What have you done when you disagreed with a company decision?

Have you ever had a time when you were supposed to take action on something, but you decided it was better to do nothing? Tell me about it.

Have you ever disagreed with a company policy? What did you do? What were the results?

How have you gone about solving work related problems at ABC? At DEF?

Give me some examples in which you have made quick business decisions. What were the outcomes?

What is the biggest business risk you have taken?

Have you ever disagreed with a boss? What happened?

SM: Self Motivation

Has the candidate, on his or her own initiative and money, *studied to improve by taking extra courses, attended night school, read books, attended seminars? Self development is a strong indication of self motivation. Speaking passionately about the job during the interview or for example, speaking of loving sales or working with numbers in accounting, or handling people is another strong indicator of self motivation.*

Why are you applying for this job?

What have you done to improve your career path since you have been at ABC? Did you pay for this yourself?

What courses have you attended to learn more about your profession?

What books have you read about your profession in the past year? Tell me some points that you picked up.

What journals do you subscribe to and read?

How do you keep yourself up-to-date in the field of………?

What prompted you to interview with us?

Why did you decide to become a(n) …………?

Why did you select engineering as a profession?
What keeps you in sales?

What have you done to improve your career in …..?

SS&PP: Selling Skills and Persuasive Power

What types of selling courses have you been involved in? Tell me more about them and how they have affected your selling?

Tell me about your biggest selling accomplishments and why you are proud of them?

Who were your most influential sales managers? How many salespeople like you did they have? Where did you rank?

How many people are in your sales force? In your group? Where do you rank?

Tell me information about any sales awards or contests that you want me to know about?

Tell me about your biggest sales achievements.

What was your biggest selling disappointment?

What do you do differently than others in selling?

Will your sales manager at XYZ say you were an A, B, C or D? Why?

What selling books have you read or what things have you done to improve your selling career? What were the results?

How do you decide on what clients to call on?

How do you decide which clients to call on?

What were your objectives or quotas for last year? How did you do?

How do you get prospects?
What kind of bonus payout did ABC have? How did you do?

Were you ever selected for special assignments because of your selling skills?

How were you rated at ABC? What did your performance appraisal say? Can you send me a copy?

Have you been promoted at ABC? Were you promoted at DEF?

When we call Mr. Jones for a reference, where will he tell me you ranked in your sales?

Were you ever promoted in the sales rank?

Have you ever trained other sales people? Why were you selected to train?

WE: Work Ethic
Does the candidate talk about being ready, willing, and able to go the extra mile to get the job done?

What will your managers at ABC tell us about your attendance and punctuality?

Tell me about your work day at ABC. (Tell me about when you regularly start working and when you regularly quit working.)

Tell me about a time you went "above and beyond" to deliver a project or get the job done. Can you tell me about other times?

Other Performance Predictors and Questions
AS: Analytical Skills
What have been your biggest challenges at ABC and how did you go about solving them?

What has been your best solution that you have presented to a company? What other solutions would you like to tell me about?

Tell me about a problem that you saw at ABC and what you did about it. Other examples?

Have you ever spotted a problem before it occurred? What did you do?

When have you discovered or been handed a major surprise; how did you deal with it?

What is the most critical problem that you have faced at ABC? At DEF? What did you do? What was your role in solving it? How did you get others involved?

AP: Attendance and Punctuality
If we call Ms. Jones for a reference, how many times will she say you were absent last year? The last two years?

At ABC how many days did you miss in the last three years?

Tell me about your attendance record and punctuality record at ABC?

Tell me about starting your day at ABC? What time did you arrive at work? What time did you leave daily?

CHG: Change
Tell me about times when your ideas have been implemented and caused change?

Tell me about the biggest business risk that you have taken and the results.

What was your biggest career decision?

What was your worst business decision? How was the negative effect scaled down?

How do you follow-up on goals?

Have you ever identified a problem and created the solution? How did you do it?

What crisis did you face at ABC and what was the process you took to fix it?

CFD: Confidence
Evaluate poise and self assurance displayed by the candidate during the interview. Confidence will also be evident when answering Risk Taking and Decisiveness questions.

What is the biggest business risk that you have taken?

When have you stepped out on a limb for your manager or company?

Tell me about the best business decision that you have made.

Have you ever been on stage? Spoken before a group?

Tell me about a time when your courage pulled you through.

What was the last business decision that you faced?

Have you ever volunteered for a project just because you knew you could do it?

What promotions have you been given and why?

EST: Estimating
Explain to me how you went about estimating a large project?

What is the largest dollar project that you have estimated at ABC? What were the results?

When did you not get a bid from your estimating at ABC? What happened?

What software do you use in estimating? Why?

FI: Firing
These questions will give you data on the candidate's judgment, confidence, and decisiveness; it also reveals the logical sequence the candidate may have followed during the termination process. If, on the other hand, a person says they never fire poor performers, it may indicate indecisiveness.

What have been your most challenging experiences with below standard performing people? What did you do?

Tell me about a time when you fired someone and how you went about it?

Have you ever identified poor performing individuals? If so what did you do?

How do you go about dealing with a difficult employee?

How do you feel after you have fired someone? Why?

Have you ever been hesitant to fire someone? Tell me about it?

Tell me about a difficult employee who stands out in your mind. What did you do about the employee?

Have you ever fired anyone? Please be specific and tell me how you went about it.

How do you document your terminations?

Have you ever had a time when you almost fired someone but did not? Tell me about it.

FLX: Flexibility
Listen to see how the candidate adapted to changing situations. Listen to the words they use describing how they felt and what were the results.

Contrast your last two managers. How did you work with them?

Have you ever gotten a new boss? How did you react?

Have you ever gotten a new management team? How did you react?

How did you feel when ABC went to the new computer system? The new….? (Generic question – insert new anything.)

What was the biggest change that happened to you at ABC? At DEF? How did you react? How did you feel?

What was the biggest adjustment that you had to make at ABC?

What has been the biggest change that you had to face at ABC?

Have you ever had an initial plan rejected and then redid it, and sold it?

What different job responsibilities have you adjusted to?

Have you ever had a plan and then had to change direction? Tell me about what you did? How did you feel?

What has caused you the most stress?

What hurdles did you encounter at ABC? What did you do?

How did you gain team support at ABC? Management support?

Do you have to manage some of your people differently? Why?

HIR: Hiring
Look at the candidate's hiring philosophy, the hiring processes they believe in and have used and the results of their hires. Did they set a goal to hire the best people even better than themselves or have they hired people who won't show them up? Also assess their general knowledge of hiring and EEO laws.

Have you ever hired anyone that has been promoted above you or to your level?

Tell me about the last three people that you hired. How are they doing?

Tell me what you looked for and wanted in the last people that you hired at ABC? How did you go about selecting them? How are they doing?

Have any of your hires been promoted?

What are your favorite interviewing questions? What are they designed to tell you?

What positions have you been responsible for hiring? Tell me about the last person you hired for the position of.............?

What must you not ask questions about? What can you ask questions about?

Tell me about the most successful employees that you have hired. Where are they today? Who was promoted?

Are they doing anything differently at ABC in hiring because of you?

What is the turnover like in the area you manage? Why?

How do you get information on a person's integrity?

What is your opinion on reference checks? Tell me about specific examples of reference checks and where you got them.

In your last three hires, did you get reference checks?

Did you check your last hires to see if they really had their degree? Tell me the steps you took to do that?

Tell me about the worst hire you've made. What should you have done differently to avoid this mistake?

IC: Innovation and Creativity
Did you have ideas at ABC that helped them?

Did you ever have the opportunity to change something at ABC? What were the results?

What were the successful new concepts (ideas, plans, and products) that you introduced at ABC?

Did you ever sell your boss or company on taking a new direction?

Tell me about some of the ideas you had that your company did not implement? Ideas that were implemented?

Do you consider yourself a creative, innovative person on the job? If yes, why?

Describe a problem that you solved by creating a different way?

What are they doing differently at ABC because of you? At DEF?

Tell me what they are doing differently at your last two companies because of you?

What is the biggest change that you have caused a company to make that you worked for?

L: Loyalty
This is also related to being a team player and loyal to company and boss. A clue to loyalty is to look for whether the candidate speaks in a positive manner or is negative about team members, peers, bosses and companies.

What did you think of ABC Company? DEF Company?

Contrast your manager at ABC with your manager at DEF.

Tell me about your manager at ABC; at DEF.

Describe to me the people that you worked closely with?

Why did you leave your last job? The one before that?

Tell me how it was to work for ABC? How was it to work for DEF?

What are your relationships like with your past managers at ABC or DEF today?

What, if any, bridges have you burned with managers in your past employment that you might like us not to contact? Why?

PD: People Development
Training and motivating your people.

Which of your employees are you proudest of? Why? What are you doing to grow them?

How is your team performing compared to other teams in the company? Why?

What would your boss say your strongest managerial skills are?

What would your team say your strongest managerial skills are?

What was the most productive team that you developed? How did you build this team?

Have any teams that you have managed ever been recognized by the company? Or your boss?

When have you faced the problem of a problem employee? Tell me the specifics of what you did to remedy the problem? Other examples?

How do you give employee feedback?

PRO: Process
What processes have you started which made positive changes in your department or company?

What are the largest projects that you have been in charge of and what did you do to make them happen successfully?

Have you ever managed for output? How did you measure it?

Do you ever monitor results after completion? What have you learned? What changes have you implemented?

PA: Performance Appraisal Questioning
Tell me about your performance appraisal at ABC. At DEF. Would you send me copies?

What will your performance appraisals say about your attendance and punctuality?

Will you send us copies of your appraisal(s)?

How has your manager rated your performance (or talked to you about your performance) in the areas of ....?

What have you been told your strong areas of performance are? Areas of performance which need improvement?

What will your manager, Ms. ....say your strong areas are? What areas have your manager Ms.........said that you needed to improve?

How was your performance rated at ABC? At DEF?

When have you been most pleased with your performance at ABC, and when have you been less than happy with your performance?

How do you know when you are doing a good job?

R: Responsiveness
Have you ever had times when you had to go out of your way to please an internal or external customer? Please explain.

How have you helped other employees?

What was your most trying time with a customer?

How have you given extra value to your clients?

When have you walked the extra mile, and what were the results?

SAF: Safety
What safety programs and safety initiatives have you been responsible for?

How have your safety initiatives helped the company's bottom line?

What type of safety training have you provided to your employees? Who *developed* this training? Who *delivered* this training?

When are you required to complete the OSHA Form 200 report? What do you do with this?

When are you required to complete the OSHA 101 Form report? What do you do with this?

When you've come upon an employee disregarding safe practices, what did you do?

Tell me about how and when you schedule safety meetings. What have been the results?

What has your facility's lost-time record been the past ….. years? Has lost time gone up or down? Why?

What are your safety credentials?

ST: Stress Tolerance

What are the biggest pressures that you have faced at ABC? How did you deal with the pressure?

When are you best at your work? When are you less effective?

When were you under the heat at ABC? What did you do?

Describe some tough deadlines that you have faced.

How do you go about meeting budget?

Have you ever had a business situation where you had to react on your feet? What happened?

What caused you the most stress at ABC? At DEF?

T: Tenacity

One of the critical Predictors for sales positions
What was your most difficult business accomplishment?

What is the longest that you have had to work on a project or sale at ABC?

Have you ever had a time when you just did not give up on a sale, a project, an idea?

What sale did you make at ABC that took you the longest?

Have you ever had an idea or plan that took you a long time to implement? How long? How did you do it?

What was your most difficult sale, project, challenge at ABC?

Tell me about a time when you demonstrated a lot of persistence?

Tell me about a business situation when you did not take no for an answer.

What has been your proudest achievement and why?

What is the hardest that you have worked to get an idea or project to be implemented?

TP: Technical Proficiency

Technical proficiency is a key reason the candidate has gotten this far in the interview process. Now, it is the other interviewing skills that distinguish the candidate from the competition. This does not lessen the value of technical proficiency, however.

Tell me about the areas in (your profession) you are most confident about? Least confident?

Explain your most helpful tool and how you use it to get your job done.

How many times did it take you to pass the CPA exam, and why did you do it?

What are the skills in (your profession) that are your best? What skills do you need to improve?

What have you done to improve your skills in your profession? How do you keep updated in your field?

V&SP: Vision & Strategic Planning

How do you find new opportunities and bring them to fruition?

How do your team's goals contribute to the company's strategy?

Have you ever spotted another company that was doing something your company should be doing? What did you do?

How do you keep current on business issues?

Have you ever had to make an unpopular decision? Tell me about it.

Tell me about the strategic plans that you have executed at ABC?

The Classics
They are not called Classics for nothing.

Why should we hire you to do this job?

This will tell you how candidates see their responsibilities and the relative importance of them with no guidance from you.

What are your strengths and weaknesses?
You could ask for two of each.

If you designed a job for yourself, what would you be doing and in what environment?

How do you see your career advancing? Do you have a goal and timeline for that goal?

What do you like, and what would you like to change about your present employer and the job you do?
A great test of character, and political agility. How to delicately "criticize" your company in clarifying what you do not want repeated— requires finesse.

Are you looking at other jobs?
Here is a great test of honesty and self-confidence. If the person immediately looks at their feet, there is a problem. Count the seconds to answer: It should be almost reflexive and immediate. Too many words from the candidate spells trouble here. Look for eye contact and a firm yes or no.

Will you relocate? Are there things that would make this difficult for you?
This opens up many avenues, going far beyond a simple yes or no. Hope for input about spouses, lovers and the kids, and think about how any of this impacts the company. This is one avenue to legally ask questions you cannot ask. Listen carefully.

What excites you about your job, and what do you expect to see more of in the new job?
It is a basic motivation question. There is no right answer.

Can you handle being wrong?

Can you take orders?

What caused you to join ABC?

What are the key strengths that you bring to this position? Explain.

What were your main duties when you started? Did they expand? Were you promoted?

What are your favorite parts about your last job? What didn't you like? Why?

Who did you report to at ABC? What would he or she say your strengths were? Areas for improvement?

What promotions did you receive at ABC? Salary increases?

Why did you leave ABC? Was it totally your idea?
What are your biggest projects going on now?

What is your biggest problem or challenge currently?

Where does your position lie on the org chart?

Who do you deal with inside your company?

About what kind of budget are you responsible for?

What level of management do you interact with?

What kind of jobs are you interviewing for and how is it going?

In regard to leadership, in your past jobs, how have you shown ability to implement change? How did you get the people to go along?

What has been your greatest challenge as a manager and what did you do?

Tell me about the most difficult employee you had and what you did?

How have you gone about assembling your best team?

What has been your biggest role in providing change? How did you do this, and what were the results?

When have you used best practices to make positive things happen?

What was your ending salary at ABC?

What will your reference verify your ending salary was at ABC?

What are your salary expectations?

What did you like about this interview? What did you dislike?
Will you send us a copy of your degree or transcript?

When would you be ready to report to work if we selected you?

With what other companies have you applied? What have been the results?

The End...Ending Questions

Last Questions buy time and should be candidate friendly. You will need three last questions for you're A, B and C Predictor Interview Guides. I believe each last question should be designed for the applicant to sell themselves and add any information that you might have missed. The last question should be announced as the last question.

Before the last question, go over your Predictor Interview Guide and make sure there is nothing you missed. Example...did you ask the candidate to send you a copy of the transcript or degree? Did you get reference phone numbers...can you read them? This is your last chance to check it out, and make sure you have not missed anything.

I have one last question. After I ask it, I will give you time to think it over while I review my notes and see if there is anything that I have missed.

My last question is the wishing well, if you were wishing that you had the opportunity to tell me about anything that I have missed your opportunity is now. What would you like to tell me?

For my last question, it is your turn to tell me anything that might help me make the decision to recommend that you be hired.

This is my last question; please tell me anything that you would like to add that might help us select you.

The last question—Is there anything we have missed in your background which indicates that we should hire you?

30

TeleScreen, Predictor Interview Guide and Reference Example Forms

I. TeleScreen Interview form
See Chapter 20—The Ten Minute TeleScreen that Works

Guidelines and Instructions for Writing your TeleScreen

Write your TeleScreen with only questions that are job related. Use the job description, job requirements and job expectations and relate these to key Performance Predictors that are critical to successful job performance.

You may want to write custom questions or use applicable Predictor Interview questions listed in Chapter 29.

Remember the TeleScreen's main purpose is to eliminate candidates for interviewing. Write only enough questions to allow you to make your decisions. It can also be used to prioritize the candidates that seem best and you want to see first.

Example TeleScreen

ABC Company TeleScreen Interview

Applicant's Name		Date	
Address		Phone: Home Cell	
	Interviewer		
e-mail	Schedule Further Interview ☐ Yes ☐ No	Date	Time
Position Applied For: Project Manager		Predictor Rating	

JOB DESCRIPTION
State the job description and any negatives.

> **The Project Manager jointly directs many workflow segments and jointly approves many decisions concerning project cost, time and performance according to agreed upon baseline requirements with the Senior Project Manager and Division Managers. The Project Manager has accountability, responsibility and authority for completing the project with the functional departments and operations departments. This job may require weekend work.**

INTERVIEW

Are you currently employed? ☐ Yes   ☐ No
If Yes, tell me a little about your job? _____

_____

_____

Why do you want to leave your current job? _____
_____
_____

If No, Please explain why you are unemployed and for how long?
_____
_____

Either in this job or your last job, who did you report to? Will you use this person as a reference?
Name:_____Phone Number: _____

If No, why won't you use this person as a reference? _____
_____
_____

What will this person say your strengths are?_____
_____
_____

What did they ask you to improve on?_____
_____
_____

What will this person say about your ability to meet deadlines? ___
_____
_____
_____

May I ask what you are currently making? _____
_____
_____

What are your salary expectations? _____
_____
_____

Why are you applying for the ABC Company Project Manager position?_____
_____
_____

What is there in your background to indicate you can do the ABC Company Project Manager job at a superior level?

_____

_____

_____

What key business accomplishments would you like to tell me about?_____

_____

_____

Is there anything else you would like to tell me about that might help us in our decision to invite you to interview for the ABC Company Project Manager job? _____

_____

_____

CLOSING

If you consider this applicant acceptable to continue in the interviewing process, say something similar to:
"_____ (applicant's name), I am interested in having you talk to us in more depth about your qualifications and accomplishments. Could you do an in-depth interview? We will be back to you this coming week to arrange this."

If you do not consider this applicant acceptable to continue in the interviewing process, say something similar to:
"We will be talking with several other applicants before selecting who we will be bringing in for personal interviews. If you do not hear from us by _____ (give a date no longer than 3-5 days from this interview), that means you probably will not. Thank you for talking with me today. Goodbye."

PREDICTOR EVALUATION

Rating	Description
5	Exceptional
4	Superior
3	Average
2	Below Average
1	Not Hirable
0	Insufficient Data

Predictor	Rating	Predictor	Rating	Predictor	Rating	Predictor	Rating
CFD		INT		JDG		POT	
CO		IPS		MS-L		WE	

Applicant scheduled for further interview: ☐ **Yes** *(fill in date and time on 1ˢᵗ page)* ☐ No

INTERVIEWER COMMENTS

_____

_____

_____

II. Predictor Interview Guide
See Chapter 18—Your Time Saving Predictor Interview Guide

Guidelines and Instructions for Writing your Predictor Interview Guide

The guidelines and instructions for writing your Predictor Interview Guide are similar to those used to write your TeleScreen. Write your Predictor Interview Guide with only questions that are job related. Use the job description, job requirements and job expectations and select the important Performance Predictors that you need data on in order to make a good hiring decision.

Write your own custom questions or use the appropriate Predictor Interview questions listed in Chapter 29.

As I discussed in Chapter 25, ideally three managers should be in the interviewing process. That way you will write A, B and C Predictor Interview Guides. The Guides may contain some identical questions in two or even the three guides, especially KO questions. The Predictor questions will be similar in that they cover the description, requirements and expectations of the job.

Usually you will develop questions designed from 8 to 12 Predictors. More than 12 Predictors become difficult to judge and lessen the probability of hiring the best. You're A, B and C Predictor Interview Guides will be used with all candidates interviewing for the position so that each receives consistent questions and treatment.

Example Predictor Interview Guide

ABC Company

PREDICTOR INTERVIEW GUIDE A

POSITION: Project MANAGER

(Interview Guide A to be completed by Hiring Manager)

Applicant's Name	Date
Address	Phone: Home Cell
Referral Source	Interviewer
Received: Resume____Transcript____Follow-up Letter____	e-mail

INSTRUCTIONS
Greet and relax the applicant. Give out your business card.

INTERVIEW
How did you hear about the ABC Company Project Manager position and decide to seek an interview with ABC?_____
_____
_____

Are you currently employed?
□ Yes. Why do you want to leave your current job?
_____
_____
_____

☐ No. Could you explain why you are unemployed?

_____

_____

_____

Who is/was your manager at _____?
What is his/her title?_____
Will you be using him/her as a reference?
☐ Yes. His/her phone number is? ___(   )_____
☐ No. Please explain why not. _____

_____

_____

On an A B C D scale, how will your manager rate you
    on planning and organization? _____ Why? _____

_____

on your attendance? _____ Why? _____

_____

overall as an employee? _____ Why? _____

_____

_____

What will your manager verify as your current salary? _____

_____

_____

What are your salary expectations? _____

_____

_____

What is exceptional in your background that would indicate your ability to do the ABC Company Project Manager job at a superior level?_____

_____

_____

When did you develop your interest in a Project Management career and why?_____

_____

_____

Tell me about critical deadlines you have had to meet and what you did to meet them._____

_____

_____

What are the major things you focus on in Project Management and why?_____

_____

_____

In the last year what has your manager said you do well in and what were you asked to improve on?

Do well in: _____

_____

_____

_____

Improve on: _____

_____

_____

Did you make any changes? _____

_____

_____

How did you learn the technical aspects of your current (or former) job?_____

_____

_____

When you have seen negative budget variances, what have you done? _____

_____

_____

Give some specific examples of what you have done to contribute to accomplishing a positive budget_____

_____

_____

When judging the performance of your team, what specific factors do you look for?_____

_____

_____

Give me specific examples of how you have resolved customer complaints during or after a project._____

_____

_____

Tell me about the time you went the extra mile for customers. _____

_____

_____

_____

What have you done on your own to improve your job performance?_

_____

_____

_____

How did you go about developing a budget for a new project? _____

_____

_____

_____

Describe the results of budgeted costs versus actual costs for the last project you managed. _____

_____

_____

Tell me about your last close out. How did you handle completing the punch list and results? _____

_____

_____

What was the most difficult project you estimated? Why? Was the customer happy? _____

_____

_____

Tell me how you planned out your largest project. _____

_____

_____

_____

Will you send me copies of your college transcript(s) and degree(s)?

☐ Yes   ☐ No

If not, why not? _____

_____

_____

(In addition, request appropriate certificates and licenses. Double check you have requested company reference telephone numbers, home and cell numbers, performance appraisals, etc.) If the candidate agrees but fails to provide, this is a red flag regarding integrity and follow-through.

I have one last question. After I ask it, I will give you time to think it over while I review my notes and see if there is anything that I have missed.

For my last question, it is your turn to tell me anything that might help me make the decision to recommend that you be hired for the ABC Company Project Manager position.

_____

_____

_____

Applicant's Questions

Now, it's your turn. What questions do you have about the Project Manager position or the ABC Company?

_____

_____

_____

Closing

> If you have not found the applicant to be hirable, say something similar to:
>
> *"Thank you for meeting with me today. We will be talking with several other applicants before making our final decision. If you have not head from us by _____ (give a date no longer than 3-5 days from today), that means you probably will not."*

> If you have found the applicant to be hirable, say something similar to: "_____ (applicant's name), I would like to have you speak to _____ & _____ (next team members doing interviews), they are _____ & _____ (titles)."
>
> Give the applicant a "brief" break while you are making interview arrangements with the next team members.

PREDICTOR EVALUATION

Rating	Description
5	Exceptional
4	Superior
3	Average
2	Below Average
1	Not Hirable
0	Insufficient Data

PREDICTOR   **RATING**

AUL:
Ability to Understand and Learn   _____

CFD:
Confidence   _____

PREDICTOR	**RATING**
CO: Communication Oral	_____
EST: Estimating	_____
INT: Integrity	_____
IPS: Interpersonal Skills (Ability to get along with fellow workers and clients)	_____
JDG: Judgment	_____
MS&L: Management Skills & Leadership	_____
PA: Problem Analysis	_____
POT: Planning, Organization & Time Management	_____
RD: Risk Taking & Decisiveness	_____
SM: Self Motivation	_____
WE: Work Ethics	_____
TOTAL	_____

INTERVIEWER COMMENTS

_____

_____

_____

III. TeleReference Guide

See Chapter 24—Reference Checking—The Validator or Terminator?

Guidelines and Instructions for Writing your TeleReference Guide

As with the TeleScreen and Predictor Interview Guides, the TeleReference Guide can be used as a template. Appropriate custom questions pertinent to the job description, requirements, expectations of the job and the candidate can be written.

Reference checking is the responsibility of the hiring manager. I strongly recommend the hiring manager do the reference checking because the hiring manager must live with the hiring decision and the employee's future performance.

Example TeleReference Guide

ABC Company TeleReference Guide

Applicant's Name	Date
Reference's Name	Phone: Office Cell
Company	Reference's Position
Position Applied For:	Interviewed By

INTRODUCTION

Hello, my name is _____ and I am the/a _____ _____ with _____ I am calling because _____ _____ (*candidate's name*) gave me permission for us to contact you as a reference. Do you have a few minutes now or would you prefer to call me back? *(My phone number is_____.)*

If the response is "*It is our company policy not to give references.*"…try the following approach:

"As a manager I understand that your only legal concerns are with a bad reference. However, if a person has done a good job for me I feel I owe them a good reference. I have no risk in giving a 'good' reference; therefore, I am happy to give them for good employees. So, I am assuming that if you are unable to give me a reference it is because the reference would be very negative. Could you help me by answering a few questions about _____ _____ (candidate's name)?"

INTERVIEW

(Only use those questions below that you feel are necessary and relevant.)
Would you please verify that _____ worked for your company and for about how long?

_____
_____
_____

Would you verify that his/her salary was approximately $_____?

What was his/her position *(or title)* with your company?

_____
_____
_____

What were _____'s principle strengths?

_____
_____
_____

What were his/her developmental needs?

_____
_____
_____

Rating him/her with your other managers on an overall basis, with C being your average manager, would you give him/her a grade of:
(circle one)　A　B　C　D　or　F　?
The reason for this rating would be…? _____
_____
_____
_____

What can you tell me about _____'s attendance?
_____
_____
_____

Using the same　A　B　C　D　or　F　scale as before, how would you rate his/her integrity? *(circle one)*
The reason for this rating would be? _____
_____
_____

Did he/she have any problems that interfered with work *(look for drugs, alcohol, etc.)*?
_____
_____
_____

Would you rehire him/her?
_____
Why?_____
_____
_____

Why did _____ leave your company?
_____
_____
_____

If you were me, would you hire _____?
_____
_____
_____

Is there anything else that I should know that might be helpful in making my decision to hire?

CLOSING

I really appreciate your help. If there is ever anything I may be able to do for you, please call me at _____ (*your phone number*).

Thank you for your time.

INTERVIEWER COMMENTS

_____

_____

_____

Your Hiring Firing Experts Notes:

31

Paullin's Points

The following is a list of *Paullin's Points* by chapter. This makes it easy for you to refer back to the respective chapter to study and understand each *Point* in more detail.

Preface
—People are the number one reason that CEOs, Executives, and Managers succeed or fail.

—You can only be as good a manager as the talent and productivity level of your employees.

Chapter 2
—Managers who can state the expense of turnover are likely to manage it. Managers who don't know their turnover cannot manage it!

—Visible Turnover Costs + Hidden Turnover Costs = The Naked Turnover Costs of Bad Hires.

—When Visible and Hidden costs of bad hires and turnover are calculated, they become Nakedly exposed expenses that can be managed to improve the bottom line.

Chapter 3
—The lawsuit is won or lost before the filing begins.

—Dollars spent on employment discrimination claims make the cost of developing a hiring, firing and performance appraisal system all based on the job description seem like a penny investment.

Chapter 4
—If you are a manager, you are not what you eat but what you hire.

—Unmotivated employees, when hired to majority, will fire the manager and the company that retains them through poor performance and poor profits.

—A company's life or death is in the hands of its hired hands.

—Bad hires are like hemorrhoids; they are a pain in the butt and must be medicated or removed.

Chapter 6
—Your performance as a manager is measured not by how you perform but how your team performs.

Chapter 9
—In addition to copies of transcripts and degrees, appropriate certificates and licenses, ask the candidate for company reference telephone numbers, home and cell numbers, performance appraisals, and anything that in your good judgment the candidate can properly handle. The candidates' time is free until you hire them, and this relieves you of the time burdens.

Chapter 10
—If you don't invest the time to do it correctly today, you will spend more time and money in repairing mistakes tomorrow.

—If there are only minnows in the pond, you can't catch a trophy fish, regardless of the bait.

—If the job requires a resume, then have three people individually interview the candidate. If it only requires an application, one or two people may be sufficient.

Chapter 11
—Include key deliverables and job objectives for the first twelve months such as reports to be completed, projects to be managed and

people to be recruited. Along with the job description, communicate these to candidates.

Chapter 12
—You can only hire to the level of your applicant pool.

—Post the job description on your company or commercial website along with the major tasks that must be completed during the first twelve months. This may screen out people who are really not interested or are not qualified to do the tasks.

—Like banks, Bonnie and Clyde would find it easy to steal employees from companies who always recruit externally. It is difficult to steal good employees from organizations who promote from within, even if more money is offered.

—Low productive and negative employees will often leave a "promotion from within company" because they constantly get bypassed. It is obvious that you do not promote substandard people just to promote from within.

—Candidates recommended by employees should still undergo the same interviewing selection process as others before a hiring decision is made.

—When you know how to do it, there are more pros than cons when hiring people away from other companies.

Chapter 13
—Ask the search firm to ask the candidate to provide copies of degrees, transcripts, CPA licenses, or any relevant documents. As the hiring company, letting the search firm do the leg work and heavy lifting allows for a generally more positive interaction with a candidate but still gets you the hard answers and facts you need.

Chapter 15
—Past job history is the best Predictor of today's and tomorrow's job performance.

—You may think that you can change a person, but stop before you get shortchanged.

—Theoretical and hypothetical questions give you beautiful theoretical and hypothetical answers that make-up a comfortable conversation. But these leave you with weak decision making data for predicting success.

Chapter 16
—Managers who hire superstars get superstar productivity, get promoted, and make the big bucks.

Chapter 18
—Having your Predictor Interview Guide as a template on your computer makes it easy to keep improving the guide by deleting and adding questions.

—Let good judgment be the deciding factor on selecting and distributing the questions in the ABC guides.

Chapter 19
—A resume is like a movie trailer which has none of the bad scenes.

—ABC Time Management: Use the ABC time management method to screen in and screen out applicants to be interviewed. Scan the resumes and make three distinct A,B,C piles. The "A" group becomes applicants that you will take to the next step. The "B" group represents borderline. After further study, then you will put them in the A group or C group. The "C" group does not qualify for the next step and will not receive further consideration.

—As a general rule: resume screen, prioritize into A, B, and C piles, then TeleScreen only the A pile.

—Look at the player not the uniform. Look at the data not the paper. Skilled resume understanding tells you what a resume says and does not say…and that says a lot.

Chapter 21
—Are you thinking about what you can't ask and all the rules? You only need to focus on the one thing you can ask about…the job description and this is a key step in successfully controlling the interview.

—Nothing encourages the candidate to talk more than silence. You cannot learn decision making information about the applicant while you are talking.

—If you just leave a little silence, the superior candidate will sense the need to start filling in the silence by sharing more information.

—If the candidate does not break the silence, that silence should break your eardrums with data. You cannot learn decision making information about the applicant while you are talking. The candidate should be talking about 75% of the time.

Chapter 24
—A bad reference check is as hard to find as a good employee. What you will hear are a lot of no comments which should raise a red flag.

—Networking Via Reference Checks: I have known executives that have called other executives for a reference check, and it has ended up in a further conversation of how their businesses could work with each other. I have also seen where the reference becomes a hire. Call this networking via reference checks.

—I can almost tell by the reluctance to talk, curtness, and tone if a manager is negative about a former employee. Conversely, good references are usually friendly in tone, and the manager wants to do the former employee a favor by giving information.

Chapter 25
—Managers should never discuss the candidate until their Predictor scores have been written down and the data sharing sessions have begun.

—The same numerical evaluation system can be used for hiring, performance appraisals, and for firing.

Chapter 26
—A manager who has an HR department as a resource and does not use it, is in the same TUNNEL OF INFLEXIBILTY as the manager who does not see how technical or management innovations can improve a business. Indeed, there is a light at the end of this TUNNEL…but, it is a train.

Chapter 29

—Remember your questions should tap the candidate's specific work experience and background. You want the candidate to tell you "what they've done" not tell you "how to do it".

Hiring Firing Experts Products

To order products go to
www.HiringFiringExperts.com
Or call Don Paullin at 847-975-1520

Or use our convenient order form on page 195

Books:
Hire Hotdogs Fire Baloney: Hiring the Best Get Praises, Raises, Promotions and Fat Profits

Hiring Hardhats: Hiring Construction People Who Build Careers, Companies & Profits

Hiring Bean Counters: Hiring Money People Who Account for Positive Cash Flow and Bottom Line Profits

Hiring White Coats: Hiring Medical People with Warm Bed Side Manners, That Heal Losses for Healthy Profits

Hiring Geeks: Hiring Computer Types That Eliminate Crashes While Increasing Speed To Win The Business Productivity Race.

Hiring Quota Busters: Hiring Sales Reps Who Make Sales Managers' Bonuses and Increase Company Profits

Hiring Firing Experts Products

To order products go to
www.HiringFiringExperts.com
Or call Don Paullin at 847-975-1520

Or use our convenient order form on page 195

CD Overviews:
Hire Hotdogs Fire Boloney: Hiring the Best Get Praises, Raises, Promotions and Fat Profits

Hiring Hardhats: Hiring Construction People Who Build Careers, Companies & Profits

Hiring Bean Counters: Hiring Money People Who Account for Positive Cash Flow and Bottom Line Profits

Hiring White Coats: Hiring Medical People with Warm Bed Side Manners, That Heal Losses for Healthy Profits

Hiring Geeks: Hiring Computer Types That Eliminate Crashes While Increasing Speed To Win The Business Productivity Race.

Hiring Quota Busters: Hiring Sales Reps Who Make Sales Managers' Bonuses and Increase Company Profits

e-books
Download any of the above titles at www.HiringFiringExperts.com.

Order Form

Fax orders: 847-303-0662. Send this form.

Telephone orders: Call 847-975-1520.

e-mail orders: Don@HiringFiringExperts.com

Postal orders: Hiring Firing Experts, Don Paullin, PO Box 440, Grayslake, Illinois, 60030, USA.

Please send the following books or CD's.

_____
_____
_____
_____

For e-books download at www.HiringFiringExperts.com

Name: _____

Address: _____

City: _____ **State:** _____ **Zip:** _____

Telephone: _____ **e-mail address:** _____

Sales Tax: Must   add 7.0% for product to be shipped to Illinois addresses.

Payment: ___Check   ___Credit Card

___Visa ___MasterCard ___Optima ___AMEX ___Discover

Card number: _____

Name on card: _____ **Exp. date:** _____

Your Hiring Firing Experts Notes:

Your Hiring Firing Experts Notes:

Your Hiring Firing Experts Notes:

Your Hiring Firing Experts Notes:

Your Hiring Firing Experts Notes: